How to Ace
Your Way Through College—and Still Have a Life!

101 Insider Secrets to Getting Good Grades for the "Non-Geek"

David Kennedy

WRP™

Wellness Research
Publishing™

Originally published in 2005 by Wellness Research Publishing™

Wellness Research
Publishing™

Wellness Research Publishing™
13900 Lake Song Lane, Suite S3
Broomfield, Colorado 80020

ISBN: 0-9772239-0-6

Cover & book design by Rudy Landry (rudeland.com)

Printed in the USA

Dedication

To my dog Albert — I miss you.

Proceeds from the sale of this book support
the Boulder Valley Humane Society.

HUMANE
SOCIETY
BOULDER VALLEY

Contents

Acknowledgments 7

Introduction: "They Laughed and Called Me a Slacker
    in High School. But When I <u>Aced</u> My
    Way Through College…" 9

Chapter 1: Why Good Grades Matter
    Now More Than Ever 15

Chapter 2: Stupid Things Students Do
    to Sabotage Their Own Success 19

Chapter 3: How to Get Your Professors to
    Give You the Benefit of the Doubt 29

Chapter 4: How to Take Useful Notes 37

Chapter 5: How to Study Smarter, Not Harder 41

Chapter 6: How to Become an Ace Test Taker 51

Chapter 7: How to Double Reading Speed
    and Comprehension 57

Chapter 8: How to Get "A's" on
    Writing Assignments 63

Chapter 9: Scientifically Tested Ways to
    Quickly Increase Your IQ 75

Chapter 10: "A" Students Share Their Secrets 91

Chapter 11: College Essentials: What You Need
    to Succeed 99

Chapter 12: The BIG Secret to College Success 107

Appendix A: Do You Make These Common Errors
    in English? 113

Appendix B: Do You Lack "Style" in Your Writing? 119

Acknowledgments

Thank you, from the bottom of my heart, to my Mom, Christine, and Dad, Dennis, for everything; to my sister, Erin, for being so supportive; to Stormy, for your love; to my grandmothers, Mimi and Charlotte, for always being there; to Linda, Jennifer and Amanda, for your love, as well; to my mentors, Bill Phillips and Sharon Babb, for your guidance; to Rudy Landry, for your A+ design work; to Corey Hilmas and Rehan Jalali, for your insights; and to the University of Missouri, for giving me a chance.

Introduction

*"They Laughed and Called Me a Slacker in High School.
But When I <u>Aced</u> My Way Through College..."*

Dear Friend,

I don't deny it.

My classmates' comments did hurt me throughout high school. Nobody really took me seriously. Peers, teachers… they saw me more as a slacker, a "screw off."

What hurt even more, though, was the letter I received one spring afternoon in 1993 from the University of Colorado, Boulder.

Growing up in the shadows of the Boulder foothills, I had always dreamed of attending CU. I remember dressing my dog Moki, a husky hundred-pound shepherd-collie mix, like Colorado's mascot, Ralphie the Buffalo. On game days, I would let Moki loose through the living room like they would Ralphie through Folsom Field. When the Buffs beat Notre Dame in the 1991 Orange Bowl, I jumped up and down as if it were me who caught the winning touchdown.

My Dad attended graduate school at CU, and I dreamed of one day following in his footsteps, roaming the hallowed grounds of the mighty Buffaloes.

When I opened that letter from the University of Colorado, and read those harsh words of rejection, it felt as if the admissions officer had just punched me in the stomach, then kicked me where it counts for good measure. The wind was knocked from me and an overwhelming rush of disappointment consumed me.

Some of the hurt was soothed a few weeks later when I received a letter of acceptance from the University of Missouri, Columbia. Who knows why MU accepted me—I had a C average and average ACT scores. Maybe it was because I was an "out-of-stater" who would be paying over $10,000 more a semester than in-staters. In any event, I'm *so* thankful Missouri took a chance on me.

Looking back, getting "dissed" by CU turned out to be one of the <u>best</u> things that ever happened to me. It was definitely a blessing in disguise and just what I needed at that time in my life because it fanned a burning desire within me to prove to myself that I was "better than average."

I remember calling my Mom in the minutes after opening that letter from MU, telling her that I'd make her and Dad proud. Although they never said it, I could tell my parents were nervous about me going to Missouri. And I don't blame them.

Out-of-state tuition was expensive, and we were by no means "well off." With student loans, we could afford it, but there was the lingering issue of my, well… aptitude for academics, or lack thereof.

Up to that point, I hadn't shown any signs that I was anything but a C student. That was cause for concern, as the whole idea of me going to Missouri was for their School of Journalism, known to be among the best in the country.

In order to even be considered for admission into the School of Journalism, you had to complete two full years of study in the main university system with at the very least a 3.0 cumulative GPA.

I hardly kept a C average in high school. How in the world was I going to average B's in college? I'm sure my parents were worried.

However, I knew I could do it. In fact, while getting a 3.0 might have been good enough to get into J-school, it wasn't good enough for me. So I set a goal for myself: Graduate from the University of

Missouri in four years with a 4.0 GPA.

Now, earning a 4.0 may not be a big deal for some "geeks" who live in the library. But for me, just an average student with average ACT scores who maybe got 3 A's <u>total</u> in high school, it was quite an objective. I remember telling one of my high school "friends," Jeff Register, about my goal. He just laughed. That only hardened my resolve.

That spring, I read about a hundred books and magazines related to "making the grade" in college. Then, later that summer, either by coincidence or by fate, I met a kid named Corey Hilmas, who shared with me a virtual "gold mine" of insider secrets about how to get good grades in college, stuff I hadn't read in any of those books and magazines.

Corey, a physics major at CU, had just completed his junior year, and that summer we'd both taken a job with the City of Lafayette (Colorado) Public Works Department. Like me, Corey was a practical joker, and we had a lot of fun that summer. After all our tomfoolery, from putting itching powder in our foreman's work gloves to clouding the cab of his F-150 with fart spray, I'm surprised we didn't get fired.

One day, Corey and I were out giving one of Lafayette's fire hydrants a fresh coat of red paint, just shooting the breeze about girls, sports, life. I told him about my goal of getting a 4.0 in college. He didn't bat an eye.

He told me, matter of factly, that I could do it. "Anyone can do it," he said. "You just gotta know how the system works... how to play the game."

Just so happened Corey himself was pulling a cumulative 4.0 going into his senior year at CU. I was flabbergasted. I thought only geeks got 4.0s. He was the furthest thing from a geek I'd ever met in my life.

"Play the game?" I asked him. "What the Sam Hill does that mean?"

That summer, Corey shared with me the most *mind-blowing* secrets to college success I could ever hope to learn. Things like how to become an ace test taker... how to get professors and T.A.s to give you the "benefit of the doubt" when grades come due... how to memorize massive amounts of information in mere minutes... how to "legally" get all the answers to final exams ahead of time... and on and on.

After that summer, Corey and I went our separate ways. I headed off to Missouri to begin my studies, and he went on to finish his senior year at CU with another 4.0, capping a perfect four years of study. We kept in touch for several years, but eventually time and distance grew between us. Last I heard, he was practicing forensic science somewhere in Maryland.

In May 1997 I graduated at the top of my class, magna cum laude, from the University of Missouri School of Journalism with a cumulative 3.9 GPA... a few B's my junior year kept me from achieving my ultimate goal. I still believe I did enough to earn A's in those courses, but that's neither here nor there. Looking back, for a kid who in high school collected C's and D's like baseball cards, I'd venture to say I did all right for myself in college.

In my four years at Missouri, not once did I ever pull an "all-nighter." I rarely studied on the weekends. And I probably averaged no more than a few hours hitting the books on weekdays. I had fun in college, and I never felt like I was "busting my ass."

I firmly believe had fate not intervened that summer leading up to my freshman year at MU, I would have been very fortunate to earn grades good enough to get me into the J-school to say nothing about graduating a few A's away from perfection. The advice my friend gave me proved *golden*.

Now, if you'll allow me, I'd like to share that advice, along with my own unique insights and secrets to college success, with you. So without further adieu, here's how to ace your way through college and *still* have a life.

Best of Success,

David Kennedy

CHAPTER 1

Why Good Grades Matter Now More Than Ever

Are you destined for a career in the fast-food industry if you fail to "make the grade" in college?

Of course not. Merely earning a college diploma is worth upwards of a million dollars, according to the U.S. Census Bureau. That's how much more the average college grad makes over his or her lifetime than someone with just a high school diploma.

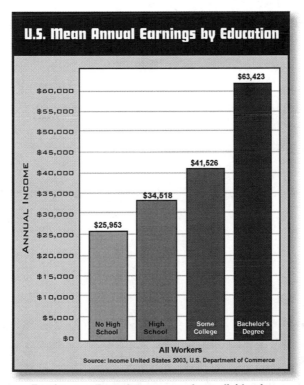

U.S. Mean Annual Earnings by Education

$63,423	Bachelor's Degree
$41,526	Some College
$34,518	High School
$25,953	No High School

ANNUAL INCOME

All Workers

Source: Income United States 2003, U.S. Department of Commerce

Earning a college degree pays huge dividends;
graduating with a good GPA pays even bigger.

That's the good news.

The not-so-good news? A college diploma, while still well worth the investment, just isn't worth what it used to be.

Consider that over 2.8 *million* people will graduate from college this year in the U.S. That's equivalent to the entire population of Chicago! Whereas a college degree was something that set you apart from the average Joe or Jane 30 years ago, in today's corporate America, you're in the minority if you *don't* have a diploma.

As it stands today, supply is far exceeding demand. According to the Bureau of Labor Statistics, there are about 250,000 *more* college graduates entering the labor force every year than there are new college-level jobs.

With such a bumper crop of college grads, you can bet employers are going to opt for the best of the bunch.

Internships, letters of recommendation, a new suit and strong handshake can help set you apart from the herd somewhat. But if you're fresh out of college with hardly any "real-world" work experience, your GPA is one of the only things you've got that speaks to your capabilities. Indeed, few things say, "I've got my act together" quite like a good GPA.

Granted, your GPA might not mean a whole lot after you've got four or five years of work experience under your belt. But if you're a new grad looking for a job, a good GPA can only work in your favor. It gives the impression to potential employers that you're different—a real go-getter, someone who takes his or her work *seriously*.

"Many highly intelligent students have lower GPAs than students of average intelligence," says Stephen Young, a former recruiter for one of the nation's largest accounting/consulting firms. "It is this very fact that sheds light on why employers *do* think the GPA is important. The GPA is important because it provides an indication of dedication to success and willingness to work hard,

A good GPA can mean the difference between getting a job and unemployment right after graduation.

both very desirable traits in an employee."

A good GPA is also important if you have aspirations of continuing your education. Try getting into any of the top law schools in the land with average grades. It *might* happen if you ace the LSAT (law school admission test), but don't count on it.

Of course, getting good grades isn't everything, and if you aren't planning on grad school, a transcript littered with C's probably won't matter much 10 years from now. But don't underestimate the extra edge a good GPA can give you right out of the blocks. It's what I call a "difference maker." All else being equal, when two new college grads are vying for the same position, the person with the more impressive GPA will almost always get the nod.

CHAPTER 2

Stupid Things Students Do to Sabotage Their Own Success

After interviewing hundreds of university students, both those who are succeeding and those who are struggling endlessly, as well as carefully analyzing my own college experience, it has become increasingly clear to me that getting good grades has a lot to do with *not sabotaging your own success*. I've discovered that many students are their own worst enemies. They do things that at the time seem innocent enough but wind up dragging their GPA down like a lead sinker does a fishing line. If good grades are something you'd like to have, you may want to think twice before doing any of the following...

1 Choose a Major Based on Practicality

I submit you'd be better off majoring in a subject you enjoy rather than something someone else tells you is "practical." Unfortunately, countless students are dissuaded from majoring in history, philosophy, anthropology and other subjects that have a reputation of not being very useful in the "real world." The late author/theologian Albert Schweitzer said it best: "Success is not the key to happiness. Happiness is the key to success. If you love what you are doing, you *will* be successful." Study something you have a passion for, and you'll not only do better academically, but chances are you'll be happier and more successful in life after college.

> **TIP:** If you major or minor in economics, be sure you *really* enjoy it—studies show economics students (majors and minors) have the lowest cumulative GPAs. Sociology students tend to have the highest.

2 Rush into Rush

I hesitate to list joining a fraternity or sorority among the "stupid things" students do to sabotage their success because there are certain benefits—for one, Greek students are less likely to drop out of school than their independent counterparts, research shows. They probably have more fun, too. But because this book is about how to get good grades in college and not "party your ass off," I'm compelled to include it.

Contrary to claims by Greek-letter society leaders that membership in a fraternity or sorority boosts academic achievement, several studies have established just the opposite—that going Greek often has a deleterious effect on grades. In fact, one recent study found that Greek members experienced an almost *four-times greater* first to second semester *decline* in their GPAs than did independent students.

Now that's not to say joining a fraternity or sorority will necessarily flush your grades down the toilet—there are countless real-world examples of Greek students performing exceptionally well in the classroom, and on some campuses, sorority members have actually been shown to have slightly better grades than the general student population. (Fraternity members almost always perform worse.) Just keep in mind that going Greek does involve a time commitment, and there are certain social obligations and temptations that can and often do derail academic success.

3 Binge Drink

Here's some sobering news about alcohol: New research out of Harvard University shows excessive intake of the amber brew can literally eat away at the gray and white matter of your brain, particularly that of the frontal lobes—the region responsible for reasoning, judgment and problem solving.

According to Harvard's Dr. Kenneth J. Mukamal, "Alcohol consumption was positively associated with measures of brain atrophy" among 3,376 adults enrolled in the university's Cardiovascular Health Study. This is concerning as it can be *years* before such tissue is regenerated, if it's regenerated at all, Dr. Mukamal says.

While the occasional drink probably won't do much harm, the kind of binge drinking that goes on across college campuses could cause significant brain atrophy, leading to a serious decline in a person's intelligence quotient (IQ).

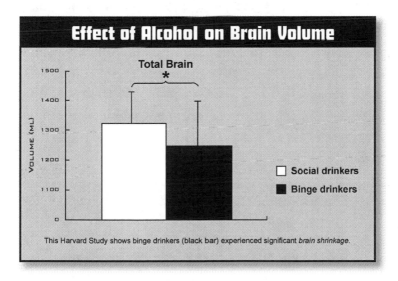

This Harvard Study shows binge drinkers (black bar) experienced significant *brain shrinkage*.

4 Get a Job

While getting a job might seem like the responsible thing to do, it can spell disaster for your GPA. Keep in mind, college is a full-time job as it is, requiring 30 to 40 hours of focused class work and study a week, if not more. Add to that 20, 30, even 40 more hours of your time working at some crummy job outside of class, and your grades can't help but suffer. Numerous studies have born this out, including one recently published in the *Journal of American College Health*, which found the number of paid or volunteer hours worked per week was strongly associated with lower average grades.

Of course, tuition is expensive, and gas and food money doesn't just grow on trees. So how else are you supposed to pay for this stuff? Through student loans and by working diligently and carefully saving during the summer months, that's how. If you're fortunate, you might even score a scholarship or two.

You'd be amazed at how much of your tuition and fees can be covered by scholarships, grants and loans. Low-interest Federal Student Aid (FSA) is readily available to just about any college student, and applying for it is absolutely free—no silly administrative or processing fees. For more information, you can visit **www.fafsa.ed.gov**. Every college and university these days has a Student Financial Aid Center—you'd be well served in paying them a visit. They'll help you determine what kinds of scholarships, grants and loans for which you qualify, as well as supply you with all the necessary application forms.

> **TIP :** Apply for *every* scholarship for which you're eligible! It's flabbergasting how many different scholarships are out there, just waiting to be given away. There's even one for students who are *left-handed*. (Seriously... it's called the Frederick and Mary F. Beckley Scholarship.)

While it's a myth that millions of dollars in unused scholarship money just sit in the bank collecting interest every year, there is a significant amount up for grabs. You're only guaranteed of not receiving any if don't apply. Forget about those smarmy "scholarship-locater services"—these scams cheat over 350,000 students out of some $5 million a year, according to the National

Association of Student Financial Aid Administrators.

Your Student Financial Aid Center will help you find plenty of scholarships for which you're eligible. You might have to spend an entire weekend filling out applications, but if you do so neatly and enthusiastically, it could very well pay off big time! Be sure to go through this process every single semester you're enrolled. Don't try once and "give up." Be persistent!

5 Skip Class

Pay heed: Skipping class, even if just a few, can get you buried nearly as fast as an avalanche victim. Given the pace at which professors cover material—sometimes a chapter's worth per class—missing just one day can cause you to become completely lost by the time the next class rolls around. That's why students who don't skip class have higher grade point averages. Numerous studies, including one recently published in the academic journal *College Teaching*, have confirmed this. "The higher the GPA of the students in our study, the fewer absences they had," concluded study authors Dr. Paul Friedman and colleagues from the Center for Teaching Excellence at the University of Kansas, Lawrence. You'll find it's easier to just go to class than it is to skip and try to catch up.

6 Be Disorganized

Being a slob can sink your GPA faster than a speeding cannon ball can a rowboat. When you're sloppy and disorganized, you miss important deadlines. Tests catch you by surprise. Papers don't get written. Homework assignments get overlooked. I recommend you keep a "master calendar" both in a personal day planner you can carry with you and also on something more prominent, such as one of those office calendars business people keep on their desks under glass. Include due dates for all homework assignments and term papers, for each and every class, as soon as they're given to you. Also include dates of all quizzes, tests and finals. Review your calendar daily—you should always be fully conscious and aware of when every test is given and homework assignment is due.

What's more, keep a separate three-ring binder for each of your classes. Forget those trashy "spiral notebooks." Take clean, concise notes on loose-leaf, college-rule paper. Title and date each sheet in the upper right-hand corner before filing it with the other notes in the appropriate class binder. We'll talk more about how to take useful notes in Chapter 4.

Finally, buy yourself a small filing cabinet (see secret No. 92) and a set of filing folders in which to keep important documents like tuition statements, class schedules, course catalogs, university mail, etc.

Forgetting about one test or paper can flush your grade for that class right down the commode. It happens to more students than you think. Don't let it happen to you. Get organized!

7 Bite Off More Than You Can Chew

Please, don't try to be a hero. Unless you're trying to graduate in three years, there's simply no need to take upward of 20 credit hours of class work in one semester—to do so will only make your college experience a miserable one, while doing irreparable harm to your GPA. Around 15 to 17 hours per semester is plenty. Anything over 18 and you're pushing your luck. Your college adviser will help you map out a course of action that will get you to graduation day without feeling like you've just gone 12 rounds with Tyson in his heyday. Which leads to the next "stupid thing" so many college students do...

8 "Blow Off" Academic Advisement

Not only should you not "blow off" meetings with your academic adviser, but you'd be smart to make every attempt to become *good friends* with your adviser. In fact, after your first meeting, send him or her a "thank you note" expressing your sincere appreciation for his/her help. How often do you suppose academic advisers receive such a note from appreciative students? If you guessed "Hardly ever," you're right on the money. Your adviser will be so taken aback by your random act of kindness that he or she can't help but become one of your biggest fans.

This is good for you because academic advisers are such a *wealth* of valuable information—they know which professors have a reputation for not giving A's and can help you steer clear of these GPA booby traps. The insight they have about professors, classes and all-around college success at your particular campus can literally mean the difference between magna cum laude and middle of the pack.

9 Be a Lazy "Ass"

A man who wanted to buy a donkey went to the market and, coming across a likely looking beast, convinced the owner that he should be allowed to take the ass home on trial, to see if the animal fit his liking. When he reached home, he placed him into his stable along with the other asses. The newcomer took a look around and immediately settled next to the laziest ass in the pen. When the master saw this, he put a halter on him at once and led him back to his owner. The latter was surprised to see him back so soon and said, "Why, do you mean to say you have tested him already?"

"I don't need to put him through any more tests," replied the other. "I could see what sort of ass he is from the companion he chose for himself."

The moral of the story, according to Aesop? "A man is known by the company he keeps."

The people you hang out with in college can have a profound influence on how successful you'll be. If you're hanging around students who don't give a donkey's fat butt about going to class or getting good grades, their lousy attitude can't help but rub off on you. Likewise, if you seek out and make friends with people who take their schoolwork seriously, their positive attitude can't help but inspire you to do well.

So, do you associate with positive people or the lazy "asses"? Take a close look at the company you keep and ask yourself if they're helping you or holding you back.

10 Study Too Much

All work and no play not only makes you a dull boy—or girl, whichever the case may be—it can also lead to a bad case of burnout, causing your GPA to go up in flames. You might consider hitting the books hard Monday through Friday, as needed on Saturday and then taking Sunday completely off. Consider Sunday your "free day"—your day to relax, recharge and forget about school entirely. This is your day to reward yourself for a successful week. (Just be careful not to have *so* much fun that you aren't ready to get after it again Monday morning.)

CHAPTER 3

How to Get Your Professors to Give You the Benefit of the Doubt

At some point in your college campaign, you'll likely find yourself in a class where you're walking a fine line between a C and a B or a B and an A.

If over the course of the semester you've been hiding out in the back of the class and your professor hasn't a clue who you are and/or thinks you weren't interested in learning and doing your best, you can be sure he or she is going to mark you down for *exactly* what you earned. If, for example, you're at 79 percent for the class, say hello to "C city."

On the other hand, if you've gone out of your way to be known, to put a face to a name, to show your professor that you're genuinely interested in doing well, you'll more often than not get the "benefit of the doubt" on everything from term papers, tests and even your final grade for the class.

Please don't underestimate this advice. It *really* can make a big difference! Here's how it works...

11 Always Sit Front and Center

If I were to ask you to conjure up an image in your mind of a lousy student—a Grade-D screw off—where would that person most likely be sitting in your make-believe classroom? In the back, right? Probably shooting spitballs or something.

Now, picture in your mind a sparkling A+ student. Where is he or she sitting? Let me guess... front and center?

It's my strong belief that students who sit front and center enjoy a number of "unfair" advantages over students who sit in the rear.

• First of all, when you consistently sit up front and center, your professor or teaching assistant gets to know you. You become a familiar face. Conversely, those students sitting in the rear often get lost in the crowd. What's more, sitting front and center sends an unspoken message to your professor that you are there to learn... that you are genuinely interested in doing your best. This can make a HUGE difference when grades are due. If your professor knows you and feels that you are putting forth your best effort, he or she will almost always give you the benefit of the doubt.

• Like you, your professor, if asked where an A+ student is most likely to sit, would probably say front and center. If *you* always sit up front and center, your professor will probably subconsciously "typecast" you as a very good student, even if you're not. This could give you an extra edge when your professor is scoring your class work, especially if subjective grading is involved, such as on writing assignments. Having "profiled" you as a good student, your professor may score your work higher than he or she might otherwise.

• When you sit toward the rear of the class, you have a lot of "white noise" in front of you: papers shuffling, students moving around in their seats, chit-chat, etc. — all this can be terribly distracting. When you are sitting in the front row, on the other hand, the focal point of your attention is your professor. In this position, you are more attentive, you take better notes, and it's just easier to stay focused.

> **TIP:** As an added bonus, your professor is less likely to call on you when you sit front and center. Professors are more apt to pick out the students who appear to be hiding out in the crowd.

12 Act Interested

According to a recent study by UCLA psychology professor Dr. Albert Mehrabian, **55 percent** of the communication signals we send results from our *body language*, while just 7 percent comes from the actual words we use.

When you're staring off into space or slouched down in your chair, head in hand, doodling in your notebook, what kind of message do you think that sends to your professor? Whether you mean to or not, it sends the message that you think your professor's lecture is *boring* and that you'd rather be somewhere *else*. Obviously, these aren't the type of "communication signals" you want to be transmitting if you hope to receive any help with your grade.

You'd be better to send messages communicating that you not only care but are *interested* in what your professor has to say. Keep in mind, your professors spend a lot of time with their lesson plans and appreciate knowing that their words are getting through. You "tell" your professors this by sitting up straight, making eye contact in between taking notes, subtly nodding your head whenever he or she makes an important point, things of this nature.

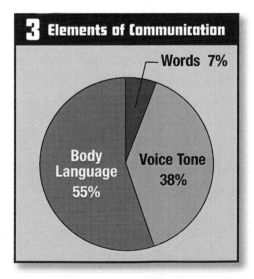

3 Elements of Communication

Words 7%

Body Language 55%

Voice Tone 38%

13 Look the Part

When I was in college, it amazed me how many students showed up to class looking like they just rolled out of bed. They'd stumble in, their hair all a mess, wearing sweatpants and a T-shirt, drinking their coffee or soda. They paid a lot of money for tuition, and they're entitled to come to class looking like a slob, I suppose. But think of what kind of message that sends to the professor. If you just landed a well-paying job and wanted to make a good impression with your employer, would you show up to work in your pajamas? If you did, what do you think your employer would think of you? Probably that you don't take your work all that seriously, right? Well, what's your professor to think of you if you're always showing up to class looking like you woke up 15 minutes ago?

Now I'm not saying you need to show up to class wearing your Sunday best. Just look presentable. Your attire should be something you'd feel comfortable wearing in church. That means no Señor Frogs or Big Johnson Spring Break 2005 T-shirts. Dress for success. Look like you care.

14 Show Courtesy

Most if not all professors these days have advanced academic degrees, and to them it's a source of tremendous pride. Earning a doctorate is among a professor's highest achievements.

The last thing you want to do is disparage their accomplishment by calling them by their *first* name… "Hey Bob, I have a question." This sends a message that you are unimpressed with their academic achievements and think of them more as a peer than distinguished college professor.

You're better to call your professors by their *last* name, being careful to flag it with the appropriate "courtesy title." For instance, if your professor owns a doctorate, you'd be well-served by referring to him or her as "Dr. Smith" or whatever.

You can usually find your professor's academic distinctions at the top of the class syllabus. If you're uncertain, preceding his/her last name with "Professor" will suffice... i.e., "Professor Smith, I have a question." Be careful to also use proper "courtesy" on term papers and report title pages, and never, *ever* misspell his or her name. Again, refer to the syllabus and double-check, better yet *triple* check, the spelling.

Teaching assistants are generally graduate students and have yet to earn advanced degrees. Still, it's best to show deference by referring to them by their last name, preceding it with Mr. or Ms., unless asked differently.

15 Go to Office Hours Every So Often

Most college professors and teaching assistants have "office hours" set aside every week, where they invite students to come in outside of class to ask questions and receive additional help. You should make a point of it to go to these every so often. Not only does this allow your professors to get to know you, but it's yet another way to show your professor that you care—that you are eager to learn and succeed.

As an added bonus, many times professors are more than happy to give you advice on how to do well in the class and will often "spill the beans" about what's going to be on upcoming tests. You'd be amazed at the amount of "inside info" you can receive by simply showing up to office hours. All you have to do is ask. Be sincere. Let each professor know that you are looking forward to his or her class and are eager to do well. Ask if they have any past tests on file from which you can study. Most do, and many times you'll find the very same questions from these old exams showing up on your exams. And even if they're not the same questions, the style will likely be very similar.

> **TIP:** Be careful not to show up to office hours too often, meaning every week. This just makes you look like a brown-noser and can backfire big time. Space it out a little. A good rule of thumb is every other week or so, or just before a big exam. And have a few questions prepared related to the class. Don't just show up to shoot the breeze.

16 Don't Be Annoying

Just as there are ways to win the favor of your professors—to get them to give you the benefit of the doubt—there are also ways to flush your best efforts right down the toilet. Following are five stupid things students do that tend to get under the skin of their professors and teaching assistants. Warning: Don't try these at school.

1. **Showing up late to class.** Professors *hate* this. It's distracting to both them as well as the students who bothered to show up to class on time. If you have trouble walking clear across campus in time for your next class, get a bike. Never show up late to class.

2. **Eating during class.** You see some students bringing chips, candy, popcorn, soda, coffee—all sorts food and drink into class. Listen, this ain't the movies. You're there to learn, not be entertained. The sound of munching, slurping and lip-smacking is distracting and disgusting.

3. **Brown-nosing.** Professors will appreciate your earnest enthusiasm to learn and participate. What they *won't* appreciate is

obsequious behavior—i.e., "chiming in" at every opportunity during classroom discussions, showing up to office hours all the time, insincere "Eddie Haskell-like" flattery. No one likes a brown-noser.

4. **Trying to "show up" the professor.** If there's anything worse than a brown-noser it's a "know-it-all." If you take offense or find fault in what the professor is saying, you'd be wise to keep your mouth shut than to try to show your professor and fellow classmates just how smart you are. No one likes to be proven wrong or embarrassed—especially a person of authority like a professor by some punk student. Like the customer, the professor is "always right."

5. **Sleeping in class.** To a professor or teaching assistant, this is one of the greatest forms of disrespect. You might as well just hold up a sign in class that says, "You and your lectures are dry and boring!" Professors like to think their lectures are educational and engaging—your "sawing wood" in class may be construed by your professor, whether correctly or not, as a personal slight against his or her effectiveness as a lecturer. This is a big-time no-no.

17 Participate, But Not Too Much

It's a good idea to speak up every once in a while in class discussions, to show you're interested and attentive, but be careful not to overdo it. Remember, most professors don't like self-perceived know-it-alls, and they delight in opportunities to put these students back in their place—for example, liberally marking off points from papers and tests.

CHAPTER 4

How to Take Useful Notes

Why is taking useful notes important? Because the infor-mation covered in lecture—much of it you won't find in your textbook—is certain test fodder and essential citation material for any paper you're asked to write for the class. Failure to take good notes will earn you average to below averages grades on term papers and leave you lost and confused come finals. Let's not let that happen to you. Here are a handful of techniques for taking useful notes...

18 Read Ahead

I always found reading ahead—i.e., doing more than the as-signed reading—helped me take better notes. Why? Because more and more, professors like to think of themselves as original research-ers—as true authorities in the subject matter they're "professing." As such, they don't like to rely exclusively on someone else's re-search—e.g., material from a textbook—when lecturing. So often-times in lectures you'll get a lot of information not included in the text—original nuggets of research, opinion and what have you. You can be certain this stuff will be on the test.

Of course, it's easier to "pick out" these nuggets if you've read ahead—if you already have a good grasp of the material in the text. Whenever the professor starts in on his or her original offerings, a light bulb will go off in your head. "Hey, this stuff wasn't in the book—I better write it down."

19 Use Loose-Leaf Paper

Spiral notebooks are for the birds. They're just sloppy and unprofessional. Besides, that sharp metal spiral always seems to be catching on clothing or poking you. Instead, I got good results taking notes on loose-leaf, college-rule notebook paper and keeping them in a three-ring binder. I kept a separate notebook for each of my classes and dated each sheet in the upper right-hand corner as I used it. This allowed me to efficiently replace sloppy notes with clean, clear rewrites. I could also easily make additions if need be.

20 Write Down Everything Your Professor Writes Down

Whenever your professor writes something on an overhead or whiteboard, you'd be smart to write this information down, too. Lists, names, dates, factoids—whatever it is he or she writes down will more than likely be on the test. Take this material down just as your professor has presented it and go over it until you know it by heart.

21 Don't Bother with Tape Recorders

After my high school graduation, I received one of those miniature audio recorders, which students often use to tape lectures. I tried using the thing for all of about two days my first semester in college before throwing the damn thing in a drawer, never to use it again. Trying to transcribe the tape was a huge time vampire, and, with all the "white noise" the tape picked up, it was difficult to understand what the professor was saying at times. Besides, I quickly found that I just didn't need it. I already sat through the lecture once—why would I need to sit through it again (by way of this audiotape) unless I wasn't paying attention the first time? As long as you're listening carefully and taking good notes, you just don't need to bother with tape recording the proceedings.

22 Forget "Note-Taking" Rules; Just Pay Attention!

The first few weeks of my first semester in college, I was so intent on taking good notes—on following the so-called "rules" of proper note taking (e.g., the venerated Cornell Note-Taking System)—that I failed to process a lot of what the professor was actually saying. It'd go in one ear and out through my pen.

This isn't good because when you go back to review your notes, it all seems "foreign." Instead of focusing so much on following the rules of picture-perfect note taking, focus instead on *processing* the material your professor is presenting. *Listen* to what he or she is saying and let it resonate. Quickly jot down key points to help you recall the information at a later date, and pay attention to your professor's cues as to what he or she considers important—including but not limited to <u>everything</u> written on an overhead projector or blackboard.

23 Be Prepared

lame•o, (lām ō), *n. Informal.* a student who shows up to class unprepared ("uh, scuse me, uh… can I borrow some, uh, paper and a pen?"). See DORK.

Every student should have a book bag or backpack well stocked with essentials: notebook paper, a calculator, blue and black ball-point pens (only use pencils when working with numbers, such as with math, statistics or economics homework), and whatever else necessary. Carry this bag with you to each of your classes.

24 Have a Positive Attitude

Try to walk into class buoyantly and ready to learn. Remind yourself how *fortunate* you are to even have the opportunity to be in school, learning, bettering yourself. When you're in a positive, *power mindset* (as opposed to a "this sucks" mindset), you're more attentive and much more likely to take cleaner, more useful notes.

25 Make "Trivia Cards" of Your Notes

As soon as you can (preferably within a few hours after class), rewrite your notes on 3x5 note cards. I had tremendous success putting them in "Trivial Pursuit" format. On the clean backside of a card, I'd write an important word or phrase I needed to remember (a name, date, formula, court case, etc.), and on the other side—the ruled side—I'd write its definition. For example, on the back of one card I might write "Gitlow v. New York," then on the reverse side I'd write, "June 8, 1925—court decides freedom of speech and of press are fundamental personal rights and liberties protected by the due process clause of the 14th Amendment from impairment by the State." I'd then go through the cards often, until I knew them like the back of my hand.

More on flashcards and their unparalleled value as study tools in the following chapter.

CHAPTER 5

How to Study Smarter, Not Harder

Here's an important point to keep in mind: In college, students are graded on how well they perform on tests and assignments—in effect, they're graded on *results*. When grading your tests, your professors don't care how much time you spent studying. They aren't going to give you "extra credit" for studying longer than another person. All that matters is the result.

When I was in school, there were a lot of students who studied harder and longer than I did who didn't produce results. Why? Because it's not *how long* you study in college but *how* you study that matters. The key is studying smarter, not harder. I encourage you, I *beg* you, to focus on *results* when studying. Here's what I suggest...

26 Schedule Studying into Your Calendar

New York University psychology professor Dr. Peter M. Gollwitzer has shown that you're up to *seven times* more likely to follow through with an intention if you make an actual "appointment" to do it. For instance, if you intend to study for two hours tonight, you can greatly increase your chances of following through if you schedule it like you would a doctor's appointment—if you write down exactly *when* and *where* you intend to study.

So, don't just say to yourself that you're going to study tonight for a few hours. Instead, you might write down, in your day planner, that you <u>will</u> study from 7 p.m. to 9 p.m. in a back cubicle at the University Library.

27 "Go to Work"

Several surveys have shown that 80 percent of the average college student's studying is done in his or her room. This is a huge mistake. Think of people who try to "work from home" for a living. Oftentimes, it just doesn't, well… *work*. It's too easy to get distracted. Instead of working, many people will find something else to do, like watch TV, eat, read the newspaper, surf the Internet, play with the dog. In order to be productive, people in the "professional world" often need to get out of the house and go to an office. The same goes for students. Trying to study in your room just isn't a good idea. You aren't nearly as effective as you could be, especially if you have an annoying roommate who's a constant distraction. Get away from the distractions and go to a place where you can *focus*, such as a library or study hall. Think of studying as "going to work."

28 Don't Study for More Than Two Hours at a Time

Prolonged periods of study are almost as bad as not studying at all. If you try to remember *everything* in one drawn-out study marathon, you'll wind up remembering *nothing*. Your brain can only stand about two hours of studying at a time—after that, it just shuts down from information overload. Time spent studying beyond that is just time wasted. Try to study for no more than a couple hours at a time, **broken up into half-hour spurts**. Bring a watch or timer and set it to go off in 30 minutes. Study intently for a half-hour, then break for five minutes—getting up to stretch, shake off the cobwebs and reflect on what you just learned before hitting it again for another 30.

29 Use Flashcards

If I had to develop a list of just a few "top-shelf secrets" to academic success in college, the use of flashcards would undoubtedly be included. Flashcards enable you to memorize massive amounts of information—formulas, equations, definitions, dates, names, etc.—quickly and conveniently. Studies show short, frequent review of flashcards are up to **three times** more effective at helping you remember important information than long sessions of cramming.

Many students are reluctant to use flashcards because "they take too long to make." However, what they fail to realize is the process of actually creating the cards—of writing down the material—in and of itself is a valuable study technique. It greatly enhances the learning process.

For best learning and retention, I recommend the following...

• Use 3x5 ruled note cards and write down *everything* you may need to remember for a test—names, dates, facts, figures, etc. As mentioned, I got best results when I prepared my flashcards in the form of "trivia cards." For instance, if there were an upcoming test about vitamins and minerals and their functions, on the ruled side of one card, I might write, "This fat-soluble vitamin plays a crucial role in the process of blood coagulation." Then on the reverse side, I'd write "Vitamin K."

• Don't be stingy when making your cards. Never assume that some tidbit of information won't be on a test because it probably will. Professors are notorious for putting little tidbits of seemingly insignificant information on tests. Sometimes I'd make upward of 300 flashcards in preparation for a test. I'd write down everything I could think of that may be on a test.

• Prepare your cards **well in advance** of the test. To save time and help increase retention, I made flashcards after *every* class, pulling material from the lecture as well as the textbook. Then I'd go through them three times a day. When it came time to really start studying for the test, my flashcards were already made, and I already had a good grasp of the information.

- Shuffle the cards frequently to avoid learning them in a particular order.
- Review them as often as you can. Beyond my regularly scheduled study times, I would put the stack of flashcards in my backpack and flip through them whenever I had a moment—whether it be eating lunch or just chilling out.

30 Plan Ahead!

One of the best (and simplest) things you can do to supercharge the effectiveness and efficiency of your studying is to plan your study sessions ahead of time. For example, make a "Major Objective" list before you head off to study. Write down the things you know you need to accomplish during the time you spend studying. Then, keep your list with you when studying and "check off" items as you complete them.

If you don't know what you're going to study until you sit down to start studying, you waste a lot of time trying to figure out where to start and in what direction to go. But, when you plan ahead, you can eliminate a lot of unnecessary idle time. You'll be amazed at how smoothly things go.

31 Study with a Sense of Urgency!

A lot of times students will go to a local hangout to study—they'll see people they know and wind up "shooting the breeze" for the better part of the time they'd set aside to study. If they'd just save the socializing for "happy hour" and approached studying with a *sense of urgency*—with an "I must get it done as fast and efficiently as possible" attitude—they'd storm through material with greater expediency than they ever thought possible.

You might consider bringing your iPod and headphones with you and listen to light, inspiring music while you study, such as Mozart—to help focus your attention as well as cue others that you're not there to chit-chat.

32 Tackle One Subject at a Time

I've never had success with "multitask studying"—that is, bouncing from subject to subject in one study sitting (e.g., statistics for 30 minutes, then economics for an hour, then constitutional law for 45 minutes). After I finished for the night, my brain felt like mush. Everything just ran together. I could hardly even remember what the heck I just studied.

When I sat down and focused my attention like a *laser beam* on one subject, and one subject only, for a full two hours, however, I felt like I was really closing in on becoming an expert on the subject.

I got especially good results doing this in preparation for a big test. While I didn't ignore my other subjects, I did move them to the "back burner" for the days leading up to a test. I didn't want anything else interfering with my preparation. On occasions when I'd have two or more tests during the same week (finals, for example), I'd keep a similar approach, splitting up my study sessions during the day. For example, between 5 p.m. and 7 p.m., I might study nothing but statistics. Then I'd go have dinner, take a shower, refresh, then go tackle economics from 8:30 p.m. to 10:30 p.m.

33 Learn to Say "No"

It's nearly impossible to get good grades if you're constantly being pulled away from your studies to attend parties, movies, social gatherings and whatnot. If getting good grades is a priority, you need to learn to say "No." Now that doesn't mean you can't go have fun—you just need to schedule it into your calendar, being careful it doesn't interfere with the time you have set aside for studying. If there's a conflict—if your friends decide they're going to go bowling, but you've already scheduled that time to study, you need to tell them to go ahead without you and hold firm. Don't cave under peer pressure like so many "jelly spines" do. Just say "No."

34 Use Caffeine

Caffeine has been shown in numerous clinical studies to help increase concentration and focus, improving everything from typing speed and accuracy to athletic performance. All you need is a *little* caffeine, however. Too much (i.e., a half-gallon of coffee) can have just the *opposite* effect, making you jittery and scatterbrained. For best results, try drinking a cup of coffee or oolong tea 15 minutes before hitting the books.

35 Eat a Balanced Meal

Your mind, just like your muscles, needs good-quality, balanced nutrition in order to function properly. That means complex carbohydrates, quality protein, good fats and lots of pure water. Eating fast food, snack food and other garbage "gunks up" your system, causing any number of deleterious effects, including gastrointestinal upset, fatigue and impaired cognitive functioning.

It's especially important to avoid eating junk food before hitting the books. It's well known that foods rich in processed carbohydrates (candy bars, soda, fast food, cookies, crackers, pretzels, chips, cereal) cause your blood sugar to spike, then crash—this crash leading to low energy and drowsiness. In fact, eating a crummy, unbalanced lunch is typically the reason for the "midafternoon slumps" suffered by so many in America today.

Instead, an hour before studying, try eating a balanced meal, comprised of a portion of complex carbs and quality protein. (A portion is about the size of your clenched fist.) This will help fuel sustained energy while nourishing optimal brain functioning. Good complex carbs include brown rice, sweet potato, oatmeal and whole-wheat bread; quality proteins include lean meats like fish and chicken, egg whites, cottage cheese and protein powders.

My meal of choice before hitting the books was a quality nutrition shake with a few memory- and cognitive-enhancing nutrients mixed in—I've included the recipe for this "cognitive cocktail" on page 89.

36 Use the "Test Simulator" Approach

Pilots don't learn to fly by just reading about it. Eventually they need to get in the cockpit and take the controls. A good, not to mention safe, way to do this is through "flight simulators," which replicate real-life flight situations.

Along these lines, I've found the best way to study for tests is to simulate real test situations by working through dozens if not hundreds of problems you think may be included on the test. Don't just read the material. Work it!

For example, if you're taking a math or statistics course, study by working as many problems as you possibly can relevant to the material you've covered in class. You can often find sample test questions in your textbook or study guide that complements the text.

> T I P : <u>Always</u> purchase the "optional" study guide when buying your books. Many times professors will pull test questions straight from that.

Oftentimes you can also find copies of past tests from your professor on file at the University Library. If available, you *must* take advantage of these. You'd be an absolute idiot not to. If the exact questions from these tests aren't asked on your upcoming test, similar questions will be. Make copies of these tests and work through each of them at least a couple times. If the library doesn't have these tests on file, ask your professor if they're available for study purposes. These are a real "gold mine."

37 Don't Take Shortcuts

You'll often get advice on how to skim material in order to save time studying. One piece of advice I once received was buying used textbooks with certain passages already highlighted. The thought being, someone else already did the hard work for me, highlighting the "important" stuff. That way, I wouldn't have to waste my time reading the "unimportant" stuff.

I came to find out quickly that this advice was about as useful as an ashtray on a motorcycle. For one, who's to say the student who had the book before you wasn't a complete moron? How did he or she know what was important and what wasn't?

Second, *everything* you've been assigned to read is important and "fair game" on a test. Thus, you'd be well served in reading *everything* you've been assigned.

TIP: I recommend buying only new books—ones free from someone else's nonsensical highlighting and underlining messes. From there, read everything you've been assigned at least once very carefully, underlining material you feel is important. I've found this is more efficient use of your time than is trying to take shortcuts—e.g., reading this, skipping that, bouncing from chapter to chapter with no rhyme or reason.

CHAPTER 6

How to Become an Ace Test Taker

OK, this is where the "money" is. In order to do well in college, it's more than important that you become a good test taker. If you don't consider yourself in that vein, take heart—anyone can learn how to do it. Acing a test is simply a matter of being sufficiently prepared. Here's how to prepare...

38 Get All the Answers in Advance

The best way I know of to give yourself a good chance at acing big tests is to get all the answers ahead of time. You may think I'm joking, but I'm not. With some investigative work on your part, many times you can "score" the answers to any test in advance. Here's how you do it—without breaking into your professor's office after-hours.

1. Check with the University Library to see if your professor has old tests on file. Often, professors will just regurgitate the same questions on exams this semester as they used in previous semesters. If the library doesn't have these tests, ask your professor, during office hours (you don't want to tip off others in the class), if old tests are available to help with your study efforts. If the professor has gotten to know you and has taken a liking to you (see Chapter 3), he or she might just share them with you.

2. Either the professor or his or her teaching assistant (T.A.) will usually hold optional "review sessions" a few evenings before the big test. When I was in school, about 90 percent of students in the class failed to show up to these. They just

blew 'em off. Big mistake! I was amazed at how helpful these reviews were, with the professor or T.A. all but *giving away* the questions that were going to be on the test. You'd be an absolute idiot to skip these.

3. Purchase the "optional" study guides that accompany your textbook, and work through all the problems relevant to the material to be covered on the test. Like I said, professors will often pull questions straight from these guides.

4. Put yourself in your professor's shoes. If you were him or her, what questions would you ask on an exam? Develop 50 such questions and study them—you'll be surprised at how many of them, or ones similar to them, will show up on your test. Trust your intuition.

39 Use Earplugs

Someone smacking his gum, coughing, tapping his shoe or making any number of other annoying sounds during a test can completely throw you off your game and cause you to lose your focus. You can avoid such distractions by investing in a good set of earplugs, available for a few bucks at your local grocery store. Look for the foam kind, which expand to fill your entire ear cavity after you insert them. They block out virtually all sounds, allowing you peace and quiet when test taking.

40 Get a Good Night's Rest

Do not, under any circumstances, cram the night before a big test. "All nighters" just don't work—you'll simply be committing the information to your short-term memory, and you'll forget almost everything you never really learned within an hour or two. Worse, clinical studies show cognitive functioning and memory are greatly impaired in a sleep-deprived state, making you more likely to forget the stuff you really did learn. Compete in an all-night cram marathon, and odds are you'll "bonk" big time during the test.

A better plan is to prepare adequately, well in advance, and get a good eight hours of sleep the night before the test. You'll feel better and think better feeling refreshed and energized.

41 Try the "Memory Dump" Method

At the beginning of the test, scribble down on scrap paper all the helpful information you can remember—names, dates, formulas, facts, etc. Then, after scanning the test questions, do a second "memory dump" and begin.

42 True/False Exams

- On true/false questions, if one part of the statement is false, the answer is "false." All you are looking for is one piece of information to make the statement false.
- Assume all true/false questions are true. This mindset will help going into the exam because now you are just looking for that one item to make the statement false.
- Look for words like "always" and "never" in the question—they're usually a good indicator that the answer is false. These types of words are called "absolutes," and there are very few absolutes that are true.
- Words like "some," "most," "rarely" and "usually" typically indicate the answer is true. This is due to the fact that these words are not absolutes and refer to a more "grey area" of meanings.
- Cross out "double negatives." Some professors use double negatives in statements for no other reason than to confuse you. In

cases where you see a double negative, cross out the negative and the prefix. For example, "Most students would not be dissatisfied with a 1.0 GPA." When you cross out "not" and "dis" and reread the statement, the answer is clear.

STATEMENT	CROSS OUT	MEANING
Not dissatisfied	~~Not dis~~satisfied	**satisfied**
Not untruthful	~~Not un~~truthful	**truthful**
Not untrustworthy	~~Not un~~trustworthy	**trustworthy**

43 Multiple Choice Exams

- Try to answer the question on your own, without looking at the answers. You might try covering the answers with a sheet of paper, then sliding the sheet down, one answer at a time, reading each carefully to see if it matches the answer you came up with. This can prevent you from feeling overwhelmed by looking at all of the answers at once and will encourage you to read each answer carefully.

- Time flies when taking a test, so answer the easier questions first. If you come to a question you're not sure about, don't waste valuable time trying to figure it out—simply circle it and come back to it later.

- Cross out each answer that is obviously incorrect. Sometimes you can deduce the right answer by process of elimination.

- Watch for the statement "all of the above": Those answers are usually correct, but... if one of the statements is incorrect, then you've just eliminated two possible answers (that specific answer and "all of the above").

- Words such as "every," "all," "none," "always" and "only" are superlatives that indicate the correct answer must be an undisputed fact.

- "Usually," "often," "generally," "may" and "seldom" are qualifiers that could indicate a true statement.
- Look for grammatical clues. If the stem ends with the indefinite article "an," for example, then the correct response probably begins with a vowel.
- "Funny" answers are usually wrong.
- "None of the above" is usually an incorrect answer.
- The longest response is often the correct one, because the instructor tends to load it with qualifying adjectives or phrases.

44 Essay Exams

- Always read through the entire exam first, and follow directions carefully. Look for key words in the question, such as "list," "describe," "compare and contrast" and "outline," which require different types of answers.
- Don't "write around" the question—answer it directly and concisely.
- Inject your essay with specific facts from the material you learned from lecture and the text—names, dates, quotations, etc. These answers are more impressive than vague answers filled with generalities. Commit to memorizing a half-dozen good "factoids" to drop in your essays.
- Write legibly with a blue or black ballpoint pen. Pencils and felt-tip pens smudge and make for a messy essay. Bring a bottle of "Liquid Paper" to correct any mistakes you might make. Clean essays will almost always score better than sloppy ones, irrespective of their content.
- Make sure your essay is well-structured and organized. A long "James Joyce-like" stream of consciousness won't win you any points with the professor.

45 Don't Be Afraid to Ask Questions During the Exam

If you're unclear about a question on the exam, don't be afraid to ask your professor for clarification. Simply raise your hand, and he or she will walk over to where you're sitting and discuss it quietly with you. When I did this, I was amazed at how many times my professor all but gave me the right answer!

CHAPTER 7

How to Double Reading Speed and Comprehension

It's safe to say that reading will comprise at least *three-quarters* of the time you spend studying in college. The amount of book work you'll be assigned is simply enormous. Obviously, the better your reading skills, the easier time of it you'll have.

Studies show the average college student reads between 250 and 350 words per minute on fiction and non-technical materials. Optimally, you want to read at around 500 to 700 words per minute or faster.

The good news is, almost anyone can double his or her reading speed by employing certain techniques (see below) and practicing them frequently. More good news: Research has shown a close relation between speed and understanding. In most studies, an increase in rate has been paralleled by an increase in comprehension.

46 Get Your Eyes Checked

The first thing you should do is get your eyes checked. Very often slow reading is related to unclear eyesight or uncorrected eye defects.

47 Shut Up and Read

Work on eliminating the habit of pronouncing words as you read. If you're constantly sounding out words under your breath, you'll only be able to read as fast as you can read aloud. Ideally, you should be able to read most materials at a pace *two to three times* that. To help avoid sounding out words, practice by holding your tongue between your teeth as you read.

48 Avoid Rereading Words

Research shows the average student reading at 250 words per minute regresses (rereads) about 20 times per page. This is a habit that will slow your reading down to a snail's pace. Besides, rereading words is typically a waste of time because the idea being expressed is typically explained and elaborated more fully in later contexts.

49 Use a Wider Eye-span

Instead of reading word by word, which slows speed and comprehension, practice reading by phrases or thought units. This will require reading with a wider eye-span, which may be awkward at first—but, with practice, you'll get the hang of it.

50 Read by Natural Light

A recent study, one of the largest ever done on natural light in schools, found students learn faster and do better on standardized tests in classrooms with more daylight. Check this out... the researchers discovered that reading comprehension scores were *26 percent higher* in rooms with the most natural light! Math scores were 20 percent higher.

The take-home message of this research is clear: Whenever possible, read in an area with plenty of natural light, such as by a window in the library or under a skylight. In the evening, read by a lamp that casts a soft light—not too dim—over your desk and reading material. Avoid bright florescent lighting, which can strain the eyes and make reading a real chore.

51 Try the "SQ3R" Method

Personally, I never used this "grandfather of study strategies." But there is some legitimate scientific research that shows it helps increase reading comprehension.

The SQ3R method, which has you "survey, question, read, recite and review" textbook chapters, dates back to the early 1940s (Robinson, 1941). Since that time, it has become the preeminent and preferred teaching tool of many a professor and reading coach. Here's how it works.

Survey: Start by surveying the chapter you've been assigned to read. Scan the title, subheadings, charts, graphs, illustrations, photographs, captions and the introductory and closing paragraphs, to get an overall sense of what the chapter is about.

Question: Both during and after surveying the chapter, note any questions that come to mind: Who is the author? What is the central theme of the chapter? What do I already know about this subject? What in this chapter might be asked on a test?

Read: Now read through the chapter from beginning to end in detail, writing down important points, key facts, possible test fodder.

Recite: Periodically pause to reflect on what you've just read—to interact with the text and seek to answer your self-generated questions.

Review: After reading through the text carefully, pausing occasionally to make notes and reflect on what you've read, go back and review the chapter again. Expand your notes and reread the chapter if necessary.

52 Get a Bookstand

The amount of reading college students are asked to do can be a real pain in the neck, in more ways than one. Poor reading ergonomics not only impairs speed and comprehension, it can wreak havoc on your eyes and musculoskeletal system.

One of the biggest ergonomic errors students make is reading in a prone position (on their stomachs), which causes neck strain and hyperextension of the spine. Another common postural mistake is reading while looking downward for prolonged periods of time, which commonly brings about aches and pains in the upper back and neck.

Reading is best done while sitting at a desk with the book propped up using a portable bookstand. The platform of the stand should have an adjustable tilt, and the height of the stand should be adjustable, as well. The goal is to be able to read while allowing your neck to be as near an upright posture as possible. You can find good bookstands for a low cost at your college bookstore.

53 CliffsNotes Can Help

If "CliffsNotes" are available on the book, novel, play or essay you're reading, pick up a copy and give it a good read before sitting down to the real thing. They'll help give you a fuller understanding of the work and help you pick up any latent meanings and symbolisms so that you're not, for example, reading Moby Dick thinking it's just some long tale about a white whale. Check out **CliffsNotes.com** for their listing of available titles.

54 Read the Newspaper Every Morning

The best way to get better at something is to practice. However, practicing your "speed reading" on chapters you've been assigned out of your textbook probably isn't a smart idea. Instead, practice speed reading the newspaper every morning. Set a goal to read, at a faster-than-you-normally-read pace, the paper in its entirety. Besides the practice you'll get, you'll also develop a wider breadth of current events, which in and of itself will make you a better student.

CHAPTER 8

How to Get "A's" on Writing Assignments

What if I told you how to write A+ term papers in no time flat with little or no effort?

Well, dream on, buddy. It ain't gonna happen. Writing research papers takes work. Aside from slipping some "geek" a fifty to write a good paper for you, there are no shortcuts. But I will let you in on a handful of secrets I used with great success to score "A's" on virtually every paper I submitted.

Now, these secrets have little to do with proper research paper "mechanics"—that is, how to organize your essay, cite references and so forth. Those really aren't "secrets." Your professor will usually just give you that information, and you can certainly find everything you ever wanted to know about proper paper mechanics at one of hundreds of Web sites, such as Purdue University's "The Writing Lab" (owl.english.purdue.edu). Rather, these secrets have more to do with adding substance and style to your writing, giving you that "extra edge" you'll need to earn that "A."

55 Be Unconventional

Think about it... your professors read dozens if not hundreds of research papers each semester, most woefully dull and unimaginative. If your essay doesn't have anything original to offer, if it doesn't "do anything" for your professor, it's going to be nothing more than "another paper." Another "C." You might earn a "B" if it's clean and well-written. "A" papers, on the other hand, are "purple cows"—meaning, they stand out from the herd in a big way.

One of the best ways to differentiate your work is to go against the grain—to express an unconventional point of view. I've found that professors appreciate students who are willing to think outside the box and who aren't afraid to explore new ideas—within reason, of course. (Your thesis shouldn't be so "wild and crazy" that you can't support your ideas in an organized and cogent manner.)

For example, say your assignment is to write a research paper on the causes of obesity in America. Instead of pinning the blame squarely on McDonald's, increased portion sizes or pure laziness, you might explore what role skyrocketing rates of stress, depression, anxiety and other mood disorders are playing in this weighty epidemic. Piles of scientific research clearly show that increased levels of stress not only spur people to eat more, but they often disrupt the balance of certain hormones like cortisol, which can lead to weight gain.

Seek to capture your professor's interest by offering him or her something original and interesting to read—you'll be rewarded for it.

56 Get Involved

In college, professors like to see research papers, not "reports" like the ones you might have written in high school. In a report, you simply collect, organize and compile information. You're an observer. Thus your role is essentially passive. Research papers, on the other hand, require a more active brand of thinking. You're no longer the observer. Once you've chosen a topic that won't send your professor to dreamland, you gather information from many different sources and develop your own position or "thesis" and develop it as no one has ever done before. You become an authority on your topic by rejecting or agreeing with your sources and explaining your own thinking as you go. Don't, for example, rely exclusively on research carried out by others if you have the time and the means to conduct your own firsthand research (e.g., interviews, surveys, direct observation, etc.). And don't yield to the interpretations of experts and critics if you see things differently. If your own research and investigation contradicts another researcher's, then that should be reported in your findings, as well.

> **TIP:** As you become more involved in developing your own sources of information, don't be afraid to use the first person ("I") in your research papers. Who better than you can explain the reason for conducting the research in the first place, the context of an interview, or the circumstances surrounding a firsthand experience? This does not mean that you should dominate the text with constant references to yourself. It does mean, however, that personal comments are important if they serve to clarify or improve the reader's understanding of your findings.

57 Use Authoritative Sources

When you do use research not of your own, make sure it's from academically credible sources—peer-reviewed journals or books written by noted authorities in the field, for example. Look for research in magazines and newspapers only if you're aiming for a "C"—with few exceptions, these sources have no place in a good college-level research paper. (One exception might be a history essay in which you cite articles from newspapers or periodicals of the day.)

One Web site I recommend for digging up articles published in peer-reviewed academic journals is called "PubMed," hosted by the United States National Library of Medicine. The address is **PubMed.gov**. PubMed contains over 12 million abstracts from more than 4,800 biomedical journals dating back to the mid

1960s. For example, if you're writing a paper on the effects of echinacea on treating the common cold, simply type those keywords into the search engine and click "Go." At the time of this writing, some 419 scientific abstracts popped up. Another good Web site for finding published research is "HighWire Press," found at **highwire.stanford.edu**. Here, you can browse journals by topic, ranging from the biological to medical to physical to social sciences.

As far as how you should cite your sources within your paper, check with your professor. Documentation methods (MLA, Turabian and APA, for example) differ according to subject discipline.

One last note about sources: Never, ever be lazy about citing them in your paper. Plagiarism means using the language and thoughts of another author and representing them as your own. Professors just don't stand for it. If you're caught plagiarizing someone else's work, it could very well result in an "F" for the class and even spell the end of college as you know it. And with the Internet and media databases like LexisNexis, it's not hard for professors today to "bust" offenders. In fact, the hunt for cheaters is a favorite pastime for many professors. Be careful to always cite your source, whether you quote directly or paraphrase. Remember, if it's not common knowledge or your original idea, you must cite the source.

58 Always Work from an Outline

In your eagerness to just "get it done," you may be tempted to start writing without having created an outline first. Don't do it. Prepare a *written outline*. How does a carpenter begin the building of a house? He first secures a plan of the proposed structure and then proceeds to build according to the plan, scrupulously following it in every detail, beginning with the foundation. Should he "blow off" the beginning—namely, the creation of a blueprint—his labor would be wasted, and his building, should it reach completion without tumbling to pieces, would be insecure and worthless. The same law holds good for any important work, including that of writing an essay worthy of an "A." Start in on your paper without having created a perfectly formed plan to systematically pursue and you will be incoherent in your efforts and will be fortunate to earn any grade north of a "B."

Now, the structure of your outline will depend on the type of paper you're writing—your professor will give you the guidelines. If not, ask.

> **TIP:** Always ask your professor to review your outline and give feedback *before* you begin writing. (Many professors will have you submit your outline for review anyway.) The input you'll receive can be like a roadmap (or a *treasure map*) to an "A."

59 Write in an Inspired State

One of the things I've discovered about writing is you can't give what you don't have. By that I mean, if you're writing in an uninspired state of mind, you'll likely create an essay that is uninspiring. I recommend that you only write when you're in a confident, self-assured, uplifted state where you feel your absolute *best*. The day you sit down to write, make sure you've had a good night's sleep, you do an intense workout and your body is energized with balanced nutrition (more on that in the next chapter).

Beyond that, I recommend you consider watching an inspiring movie to help stimulate your positive emotions—to bring them out of the subconscious mind, so you can put them down on paper. One movie I recommend, especially for writers, is called *Finding Forrester*. Released in 2000, the film follows the story of a boy named Jamal, a basketball player and gifted student whose writing talent is nurtured by a famously reclusive author. You can rent *Finding Forrester* at Blockbuster, West Coast Video, Hollywood Video and other video stores. Or, you can purchase it through Amazon.com on DVD or on video. It's one of those films worth owning because, at least for me, it never fails to uplift.

Another thing that can help lift your spirits and clear your mind before you write your essay is to listen to music. Feel free to listen to any type of music you find uplifting, but I have one recommendation: Mozart. Throughout college, and even to this day, whenever I sit down to write something, I play the music of Mozart in the background. Some research shows the effect of Mozart's music may enhance creativity. Surprisingly, no other classical composer's work produces anything close to the "Mozart Effect." Not Bach, not Beethoven, not Strauss. The work of Mozart's shown to have the most dramatic effect is the *Sonata for Two Pianos* (K. 448), which you can find at any music store or online at Amazon.com.

60 Teach, Don't "Tell"

When writing your paper, keep in mind its purpose, which is to teach the reader what you've discovered and even persuade him or her to your point of view. I don't know about you, but the teachers I learned the most from were those who *showed* me something in a lively and interesting manner rather than "told" me matter-of-factly. Don't, for example, simply state in a paper that the number of fast-food restaurants in America is growing at a staggering pace when you can **show** this more vividly:

> *Thirty years ago, America's fast-food industry amounted to all of a scattering of hot dog stands at amusement parks and flea markets. Today, an army of burger joints, taco huts and piz-*

zerias, having already commandeered any last-remaining real estate on our city blocks, have now infiltrated our gas stations, high schools, even our hospitals. The sheer number of these restaurants is staggering.

Consider... if you set out to have a hamburger at a different McDonald's restaurant a day until you dined at every Golden Arches in America, how long would you guess it'd take you?

A year, two years, maybe five? Try 35 years! And that's just McDonald's. In sum, there are 233,000-plus fast-food restaurants littering the American landscape, bringing in an estimated $142 billion annually—more than the gross domestic product of 136 world countries.

61 Add Style

See Dick sit down at the computer. See Dick write. See professor laugh reading Dick's "grade-school-like" essay. See Dick get a "D." Don't be a Dick. Add some *style* to your writing. One way to do this is by carefully **combining sentences**. For example, consider the following...

The idea of restricting carbohydrates for purposes of weight loss is nothing new. It has been around for 140 years. The concept is in the midst of a fanatical resurgence. This resurgence is being fueled by the rising tide of obesity. It's further being fueled by the plethora of low-carb diet books, the sensationalistic attention they've received from the media and celebrities, and the promotion of these plans by food manufacturers and restaurant chains.

When you break thoughts into short sentences like this, without effective connections, it makes it look as if you're either writing for a grade-school audience or you're a grade-schooler yourself. Here's the same passage revised:

> *While the idea of restricting carbohydrates for purposes of weight loss has been around for nearly 140 years, the concept is in the midst of a fanatical resurgence, fueled by the rising tide of obesity and further by the plethora of low-carb diet books, the sensationalistic attention they've received from the media and celebrities, and the promotion of these plans by food manufacturers and restaurant chains.*

Writing metaphorically also adds style to your writing. A metaphor can connect an idea or an image in your writing to something new and unexpected and create a powerful picture for your readers. For example, don't say "Dr. Robert Atkins launched another attack on carbohydrates with the release of his updated *New Diet Revolution*" when you can say "Dr. Atkins, with all the stubborn doggedness of Captain Ahab hunting the white whale, hurled another harpoon at the white bagel and just about every other food containing carbohydrates with the release of his updated *New Diet Revolution*."

Using *italics* to emphasize certain key points can give punch to your text. Be careful not to overdo it, though. All emphasis equals no emphasis. When you try to emphasize *everything* in your text with italics, you end up emphasizing *nothing*.

Pruning unnecessary words and sentences from your text like a gardener does dead stems from a plant substantially increases the health of your writing. For example, don't say "A gentleman by the name of Dr. Jonas Salk developed and introduced the vaccine for the malady usually referred to in the vernacular as polio in the year 1955" when you can simply say "Dr. Jonas Salk developed and introduced the vaccine for polio in 1955."

62 Follow the Rules

Some professors have their own quirky "style rules" just so they can deduct points from students who fail to follow them. Just as a judge won't hesitate to mark points of a gymnast who steps out of bounds during a floor routine, professors won't think twice about marking points off your paper if you "step out of bounds" by setting the margins too wide, using the wrong font, single spacing instead of double spacing your paper, etc. If nothing of this nature is outlined in the class syllabus, it's important you ask your professor what style rules he or she would prefer you use. In terms of documentation, those who write papers in the social sciences—psychology, sociology, anthropology, political science, education, journalism or public health—usually refer to the style guidelines found in the *Publication Manual of the American Psychological Association* (APA).

63 Have Your Papers Professionally Proofread

It doesn't matter if you've just written a masterpiece—if your paper is strewn with misspellings, punctuation mishaps and other grammatical mistakes, you're not getting an "A." Period.

After all the time and effort you've invested researching, writing and rewriting, you owe it to yourself to finish the job and see to it that your paper is proofread and polished. If your proofreading proficiency leaves a lot to be desired, you might consider hiring an

English major or proofreading professional to do the dirty work for you. It really doesn't cost that much and believe you me, it makes a **huge** difference in the eyes of your professors. Most of the papers professors see are so sloppy that a crisp, clean one can't help but stand out and impress.

You'll often see English majors advertising their proofreading services in the classified section of your college newspaper. Also be sure to check out Appendix A at the back of this book: "Do You Make These Common Errors in English?"

64 Use 100 Percent Cotton Résumé Paper

Just as you wouldn't show up to a job interview wearing pajamas, your essay shouldn't show up in your professor's inbox wearing cheap paper. Instead, dress it up, make it *look* and *feel* professional by using high-quality, 100 percent cotton résumé paper, available at any office supply store.

Put yourself in your professor's shoes for a moment. Imagine having two essays in front of you: one printed on inexpensive multipurpose printer/fax paper and the other printed on thick, high-quality, textured résumé paper. Without reading them, which of the two would you assume to be the better of the two essays? The one printed on nice paper, right? Unlike grading multiple-choice or true/false tests, grading essays and research papers is a highly subjective process. I'd submit the simple act of printing your essay on professional paper could boost your score as much as a full letter grade by raising your professor's overall impressions of your work.

I always got excellent results using either plain white or off white 100 percent cotton résumé paper, but I wouldn't go any darker than that. And what about those clear plastic "report covers" as a final touch? *Don't even think about it.* I've discovered most professors hate them—and for good reason. They're amateurish and do nothing but ruin the professionalism of your paper. A simple staple in the upper left-hand corner is the only other thing you need.

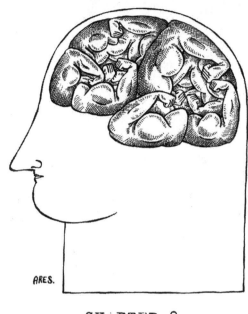

ARES.

CHAPTER 9

Scientifically Tested Ways to Quickly Increase Your IQ

Believe it or not, new scientific research is showing there are things you can do, starting today—starting *right now*, in fact—that can make you smarter. Smarter as in increased intelligence, improved memory and better all-around brain functioning.

Unfortunately, new scientific research is also showing there are simple, surprising things you can do that can make you a lot dumber. Dumber as in impaired brain functioning or "the slows." (Maybe you, like so many college students today, do some of these "dumb" things... if so, we need to nip it in the bud, fast.)

If you cut down on things that make you dumb and start doing more of the things that make you smart, do you think that it might help your academic performance?

Does a bear do business in the woods?

Of all the secrets to college success, this has got to be the biggest "no brainer," yet it amazes me how many so-called "College Survival Guides" overlook the importance of nourishing brain health.

A strong mind is to a college student what strong muscles are to a competitive weightlifter. Not only do these lifters "push iron," but they pay careful attention to proper nutrition, supplementation, sleep, everything that goes into building stronger muscles.

By the same token, any student who wishes to do well in the classroom would be smart to pay careful attention not only to his or her studies but to the other things that go into building a stronger brain.

Following is some good, wholesome, scientifically tested *food for thought*.

65 Don't Cut Carbs

In case you haven't noticed, low-carb diets are all the rage right now. Low-carb diet books litter the bestseller lists. Grocery store aisles are lined with everything from low-carb bread to breakfast cereal. Fast-food restaurants offer burgers without the bun. I think you might even be able to get low-carb hemorrhoid cream, but I'm not sure.

Make no mistake about it, low-carb diets are more pervasive than potheads at a Grateful Dead concert, but recent research is showing a carb deficit can really fog up your brain, which is the last thing a college student like yourself needs.

You see, no way of eating more alters your "brain chemistry" than does a very low-carbohydrate diet, for it forces a switch in your brain's very source of energy. Normally, your brain burns glucose (a sugar derived from carbohydrates) exclusively for fuel.

When you deprive your body of carbohydrates, something called "ketone bodies" are formed from the breakdown of fat—these ketone bodies, then, are used by the brain as a replacement source of energy. Low-carb proponents say this process, called "ketosis," is a safe, natural response in humans—a survival benefit rooted in times when periodic starvation was a normal state during the evolution of the hunter-gatherer. Furthermore, not only is ketosis safe, advocates say, but it may have therapeutic value in treating certain neurological diseases, including epilepsy, Alzheimer's, Parkinson's and even brain cancers. No question, positive research is emerging in this regard. However, the research isn't so promising with reference to low-carb diets and their effects on thinking and memory.

In what's thought to be the first, and thus far only, published study looking into the effects of a ketogenic weight-loss diet on cognitive function in humans, Dr. Rena R. Wing and her colleagues from the University of Pittsburgh School of Medicine randomly assigned 21 women to receive either a ketogenic or balanced diet that provided identical amounts of calories and protein. The women remained on the diet for 28 days.

Brain function was evaluated at least four times a week throughout the study's duration. At each cognitive assessment, the subjects completed a battery of standardized tests measuring attention and mental flexibility. While the two diet conditions produced comparable weight losses over the 28-day study—around 18 pounds—the researchers noted "highly significant" differences in cognitive functioning. Specifically, in a trail-making task "requiring higher order mental processing and flexibility," Dr. Wing and her colleagues found "there was a general tendency for subjects in the ketogenic diet group to experience worsening in performance... whereas subjects in the nonketogenic diet group showed a general pattern of improved performance."

The charts below illustrate the researchers' findings.

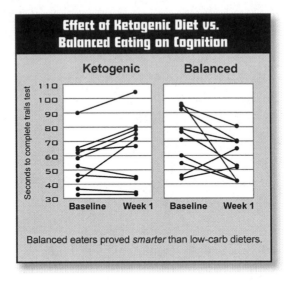

As you'll notice in the chart, the women on the balanced diet showed a trend toward improved performance on the trail-making task—they were able to complete the task more quickly throughout the first week on the diet, as would normally be expected. On the other hand, the women on the ketogenic diet showed a trend toward *decreased* performance. Throughout the first week on the diet, each time they carried out the trail-making task, their performance got progressively worse.

Low-carb diets may further erode cognitive functioning by way of elevated saturated fat intake. A 2003 paper published in the *American Journal of Clinical Nutrition* found higher proportions of saturated fats "were associated with greater risk of cognitive decline." A separate study published in the *International Journal for Vitamin and Nutrition Research* found diets high in total fat and saturated fat "were associated with an increased risk of dementia..." Another study by University of Toronto researchers found "that cognitive impairment is directly associated with saturated fatty acid intake."

Controversy swirled over a 2004 report in the *New York Times* stating that the director of research and education for Atkins Nutritionals was now telling health professionals that only 20 percent of dieters' calories should come from saturated fat. Atkins Nutritionals promptly issued a press release claiming the *Times* article and the subsequent publicity "is yet another dramatically inappropriate example of the media reporting on the media and perpetuating a false report on Atkins." The company vehemently denied it was "retreating from its long-held position on the consumption of fat," noting that "saturated fat remains a valuable part of the Atkins Nutritional Approach."

To me, this is concerning in light of growing evidence linking high intakes of saturated fat with impaired brain functioning.

The bottom line is, low-carb diets should be *avoided* at all costs by any college student wanting to maximize his or her mental capabilities. This diet is not all it's cracked up to be, and research is beginning to bring to light its many dangers and downfalls. Basic nutrition, balanced in high-quality protein, carbohydrates, essential fats, water and vitamins and minerals, has been shown, time and time again, to be the absolute *best* for brain functioning.

66 Load Up on Blueberries

If there were ever a "superfood" for the brain, blueberries may be it. New research is showing these blue little bulbs are bursting with neuro-enhancing nutrients—over a hundred per berry, in fact. Ounce for ounce, that's more than any other fruit or vegetable by a country mile. Among these nutrients are scores of antioxidants—chemical compounds that help ward off heart disease and cancer as well as enhance cognitive functioning.

"What blueberries do is what simply can be called strengthening the brain," says Dr. James Joseph, a researcher at the U.S. Department of Agriculture Human Nutrition and Research Center on Aging at Tufts University. "Blueberries have compounds that boost neuron signals and help turn back on systems in the brain that can lead to using other proteins to help with memory or other cognitive skills."

Greater memory and cognitive skills... what college student worth his or her salt wouldn't want those benefits? And all it takes is a handful of these flavor-packed juicy fruits a day.

67 Exercise Daily

The link between a strong body and mind has been recognized for ages. The ancient Greeks were convinced that only when a harmonious balance between intellect and physical development was reached could a person unlock his or her true potential. This philosophy is reflected in a phrase admiring Romans used to describe the Greeks: "Mens sana in corpore sano," which means "a sound mind in a sound body."

A team of researchers at the University of Illinois in Urbana-Champaign has recently demonstrated *quantitatively* what the early Greeks knew *intuitively*. Dr. Chuck Hillman and colleagues recently reported at the annual meeting of the Society of Psychophysiological Research in Montreal, Canada, that it's true—strengthening the body through regular exercise does indeed seem to strengthen the mind.

In the study, Dr. Hillman and colleagues, using an electroencephalogram (EEG), measured the thinking ability of 20 men and women asked to perform a computer test before and 30 minutes following fairly rigorous treadmill running. According to Dr. Hillman, exercising increased the speed of the decision-making process by an average of 35 milliseconds—quite a significant improvement as far as brain activity goes. What's more, study participants answered test questions more accurately after exercise than they did when they had not exercised.

The good news is, you don't need to spend all day in the gym to take advantage of the cognitive-enhancing effects exercise provides—30 minutes a day is all it takes. I prefer working out first thing in the morning. Not only does research show you get better fat-burning effects by working out in the morning, but it's a great way to "clear the cobwebs" from your brain and really get the day off to a great start!

68 Try Tyrosine

When it comes to natural neurotransmitter precursors, or "focus nutrients," the amino acid tyrosine may be king of the hill. Tyrosine is a direct precursor to the neurotransmitters dopamine, norepinephrine and epinephrine. It has been estimated that nearly 90 percent of these brain neurotransmitters are synthesized directly from naturally occurring tyrosine.

Studies have shown that a combination of physical and mental stress (studying is a form of stress) can lead to significant decreases in norepinephrine levels in the brain, and norepinephrine is an extremely important neurotransmitter in muscular contraction, mental focus, motivation, etc. Studies have demonstrated that when norepinephrine levels are "running low," secondary to stressful events, there is a direct correlation between that depletion and a decrease in cognitive performance. Because supplementing with tyrosine can restore norepinephrine levels, researchers believe it may be particularly effective at boosting brain power.

One study which addressed this issue a few years back strongly demonstrated that supplementing with a few grams of tyrosine significantly reduced stress-related decreases in both mood and performance.

The military has also studied tyrosine extensively. Their main interest is in how tyrosine can boost mental and physical performance under stressful conditions. Scientific papers, published by the military, assessing the effects of tyrosine as an aid to stress resistance and increased performance among troops, strongly support the idea that supplemental tyrosine can delay fatigue and increase cognition.

To see how well tyrosine would work in athletes, Dr. Jeff Stout and colleagues recently conducted a pilot study. The researchers recruited 14 male and female subjects. Half of them received 3 grams of tyrosine, and the other half received 3 grams of a cornstarch placebo (neither group knew if they were taking a placebo or the "real thing"), one hour before being put through a series of muscular endurance and strength tests. Dr. Stout notes that he really didn't expect to see much of an effect, but to his surprise, the differences were incredibly pronounced and statistically significant.

Every subject in the tyrosine group showed substantial increases in strength and endurance after only one 3-gram dose, while the placebo group showed no statistically significant change.

The chart on the following page shows the astounding differences between the placebo group and the tyrosine group. Notice the 283 percent greater muscular power generated by the tyrosine group; of course, additional studies are needed to confirm these findings, but these preliminary results offer evidence that tyrosine may significantly boost training performance by way of boosting training *focus*.

> TIP: For a pre-study boost, try taking 500 milligrams to 1,000 milligrams, 30 minutes prior to hitting the books. You can find quality tyrosine supplements at most fine health-food stores.

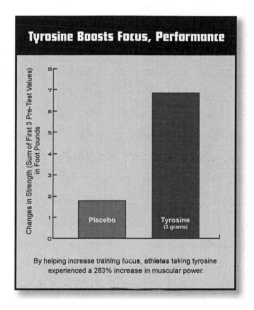

Tyrosine Boosts Focus, Performance

By helping increase training focus, athletes taking tyrosine experienced a 283% increase in muscular power.

69 Tea it Up

Drinking a few cups of green tea daily could prove to be a smart move—literally. Scientific studies continue to show the nutrients in tea nurture brain health and function.

Among the latest of these studies comes from a team of researchers in the United Kingdom, who found that tea, particularly green tea, inhibits the activity of the same enzymes in the brain that impair learning and memory and which may ultimately lead to Alzheimer's disease later in life.

According to Dr. Ed Okello, a researcher at the University of Newcastle in the U.K. and the study's lead author, the findings show tea consumption could boost the memory and learning skills of everyday drinkers. Other recent studies have shown tea consumption may improve cognition and focus. Another report published in the academic journal *Psychopharmacology* notes tea drinking "largely prevented the steady decline in alertness and cognitive capacity," which commonly occurs during the course of the day.

70 Use Creatine

We've all heard of creatine—the sports supplement that athletes eat like candy. Well, some interesting new research is showing creatine may pump up brain power as much as it does muscles.

During a recent visit to Colorado, Dr. Roger Harris, a professor at the United Kingdom's University College of Chichester and one of the world's leading creatine researchers, explained to me that he "loads up" on creatine in the days before needing to write an important research paper. He said he was sure the supplement increases mental power and focus. "We're on the verge of a whole new frontier in creatine supplementation," Dr. Harris told me.

In the wake of research coming up from "down under," Dr. Harris' prognostications are beginning to ring with profundity.

Research undertaken by scientists at Australia's University of Sydney and Macquarie University has shown that supplementing with creatine can indeed give a significant boost to working memory and general intelligence.

"We know that creatine plays a pivotal role in maintaining energy levels in the brain," says Dr. Caroline Rae, who led the research. "So it was a reasonable hypothesis that supplementing a diet with creatine could assist brain function."

In particular, Dr. Rae and colleagues discovered that supplementing with 5 grams of creatine a day for six weeks increased subjects' ability to remember long numbers, like telephone numbers, from an average number length of about seven to an average of 8.5 digits. The speed at which the brain operated was also improved, leading Dr. Rae to surmise, "Creatine supplementation may be of use to those requiring boosted mental performance in the short term—for example university students."

More good news: Over a hundred university studies have now

shown creatine supplementation to be absolutely safe. I've been using creatine myself for over seven years now and have noticed both an increase in my fitness and ability to focus. For best results, you might follow the same regimen the subjects in Dr. Rae's research study followed—that is, 5 grams of creatine daily. The supplement is widely available at both grocery and health-food stores.

71 Drink 10 Glasses of Water Daily

You could be the most dedicated student and spend hours hitting the books each week, but if you're not getting enough water, a lot of the benefits from your hard work can go right down the drain. In fact, according to Susan Kleiner, Ph.D., R.D., one of the world's leading experts in the field of human hydration, many college students are currently operating under a liquid deficit—and the consequences can be serious.

In a study published in the *Journal of the American Dietetic Association*, Dr. Kleiner reviewed the current research on fluid needs and fluid intakes and found that many Americans come up short. Her findings have been corroborated by a number of recent nationwide surveys. One conducted by the Nutrition Information Center finds Americans average only 4.6 cups of water daily—a far cry from the 10 recommended for optimal hydration. To make matters worse, results from another survey carried out recently in 14 major U.S. cities showed that Americans are countering the positive effects of the little water they are getting by drinking an average of 5.9 servings daily of diuretic or dehydration-promoting beverages such as coffee, alcohol and soda.

Based on these estimates, most college students may be walking around in a chronic state of dehydration, which does nothing but impair brain functioning.

According to a recent study published in the *European Journal of Clinical Nutrition*, even short periods of fluid restriction, leading to a loss of just 1 to 2 percent of a person's bodyweight, can lead to decreased alertness and ability to concentrate as well as increases in self-reported tiredness and headache.

In another recent study from researchers at the St. Louis University Health Sciences Center, "deteriorating mental performance" was found to be a common side effect of mild dehydration.

Because brain gray matter is made up of nearly 80 percent water, it's critical you keep yourself hydrated—Dr. Kleiner recommends drinking at least 10 tall glasses of water daily and drinking an extra glass of water for every caffeinated beverage you consume during the day.

72 Get 8 Hours of Sleep Per Night

Have a big test coming up? Thinking about pulling an all-night, caffeine-induced study marathon? If so, you might want to seriously reconsider—seems sleep deprivation benefits the brain about as much as sniffing glue, according to new research from Germany.

Scientists at the University of Luebeck in Germany found that volunteers taking a simple math test performed *three times* better when they had eight hours of sleep the night before. "A single study never settles an issue once and for all, but I would say this study does advance the field significantly," said Dr. Carl E. Hunt, director of the National Center on Sleep Disorders Research at the National Institutes of Health. "It's going to have potentially important results for students for school performance and for adults for work performance."

Dr. Jan Born, who led the study, said the results support biochemical studies of the brain that indicate memory, creativity and problem solving are enhanced during sleep, particularly during "slow wave" or deep sleep.

"Even gradual decreases in the total time for slow-wave sleep and deep sleep is correlated to a kind of decrease in memory function," Dr. Born said.

History is dotted with incidents where artists and scientists have awakened from a deep sleep to make their most notable contributions after long periods of frustration. For example, that's how Russian chemist Dmitri Mendeleev established the periodic table of elements and British poet Samuel Taylor Coleridge wrote his epic *Kubla Khan.*

73 Eat a Balanced Breakfast

Eating a good, balanced breakfast every single morning is another smart move. Studies have found that college students who consistently eat breakfast outperform non-breakfast eaters on exams. One reason for this is skipping your morning meal leads to low blood sugar, which is known to have a very detrimental effect on memory, concentration and cognition.

Before you go load up on Cocoa Puffs, however, it's important to know that not any old breakfast will bolster brain power. The kind of breakfasts most Americans eat—those so-called "continental" breakfasts loaded with processed carbohydrates like juice, bagels and sugary cereal—could be just as bad for your brain as not eating at all. You see, unbalanced meals top-heavy in refined carbs cause a "spike" then "crash" in your blood sugar levels. Often this resultant crash causes your blood sugar to dip to levels lower than before you even ate. Obviously, this isn't good considering the deleterious effects of low blood sugar on brain function.

So what kind of breakfasts are best? Those balanced in protein, carbohydrates and good fats, according to the bulk of the scientific literature. One 2004 study published in the *American Journal of Clinical Nutrition* found that dietary protein, carbohydrates and fat all play an important role in memory and cognition, and people who skimp on these essential macronutrients are likely not living up to their cognitive potential.

"To our knowledge, the present study is the first to show that pure dietary protein, carbohydrate and fat all enhance memory," says lead study author Dr. Randall J. Kaplan, a professor of nutrition science at the University of Toronto. "The finding that protein and fat enhanced memory was novel, whereas the benefits of glucose are supported by numerous studies in humans and animals."

And the effects are immediate, Dr. Kaplan reports. After fasting overnight, 11 men and 11 women consumed a breakfast consisting of either a nutrition shake containing whey protein, carbohydrates and essential fats or a non-energy placebo on four separate mornings. Cognitive tests were administered 15 and 60 minutes after ingestion of the drinks. Compared with the placebo, all three macronutrients (protein, carbs and fat) improved recall and memory within 15 minutes after ingestion, says Dr. Kaplan.

Utilizing the latest scientific research related to "neuro nutrition," I've devised what I believe to be one of the smartest breakfasts any college student could ever hope to consume—a sort of "cognitive cocktail" sure to bolster brainpower. I encourage you to give it a try... it's absolutely delicious, and I've really noticed a big difference in my ability to focus since I've been consuming it for breakfast myself.

"The Ultimate Cognitive Cocktail"
Sweet, smooth blueberries blended with
brain-bolstering nutrition!

Servings: 1
Preparation Time: 3 minutes

Ingredients
1 cup cold water
1 scoop (about 24 grams of protein)
  vanilla protein (whey or soy)
2 Tbsp frozen orange juice concentrate
10 frozen blueberries
5 grams creatine monohydrate powder
3 ice cubes

Directions
1 Pour cold water in blender. Then
  add protein powder and blend on
  medium speed for 15 seconds.

2 Add frozen orange juice concentrate,
  blueberries and creatine; blend 30
  more seconds. Add ice cubes and
  blend on high speed until smooth,
  about 30 more seconds.

3 Pour into a tall glass, serve
  and enjoy!

CHAPTER 10

"A" Students Share Their Secrets

In researching this book, I interviewed 140 college seniors pulling a cumulative GPA of at least 3.7 or higher. My goal was to get a good sampling of students from schools spanning the countryside—included among those, Harvard, Cal Berkeley, Mizzou, Minnesota, USC, Princeton, UT-Austin, Tennessee, Ohio State and Notre Dame. I asked these students to share their "unconventional advice" for succeeding in college. Here's some of what they told me...

74 Drop it Like it's Hot

"If you find yourself in a class that's way over your head, just drop it. My sophomore year, I enrolled in an advanced-level economics course that I wasn't ready for. I knew it after the first day. The professor might as well have been speaking Chinese—I didn't have a clue what he was talking about. After class, I went straight to see my academic adviser to go over my options. I dropped the class and was able to get into a religious studies course instead. It was one of the best moves I ever made.

"If you have a bad feeling about a certain class on your schedule, go talk with your adviser about dropping it. You need to act fast, though, if you want to replace it with something else—usually within the first week. And NEVER drop a class before talking with your adviser first."

—Kimberly, Religious Studies
University of Texas,
Austin

75 Procrastinate at Your Own Peril

"What helped me the most in college was breaking my bad habit of procrastinating. I used to put everything off, and it really screwed me my freshman year. I couldn't get into two classes I wanted to take because I registered on the last day you could. After that, I started mapping out my next semester, with the help of my academic adviser, at least a few weeks before registration. Then, on the very first day of registration, I got it all taken care of. Procrastination just leads to a lot of unnecessary stress and makes your life in college more difficult than it needs to be. If you have a bad habit of putting things off, I recommend the book *Getting Things Done: The Art of Stress-Free Productivity* by David Allen. I found it very helpful."

—Scott, Engineering
Ohio State University

76 Read Your Mail

"Read your university mail. All of it. When I first started at Mizzou, I received all kinds of mailings from the university—I threw most of it out, thinking it was just junk mail, like maybe they were writing to tell me textbooks were now 30 percent off at the University Bookstore. One of the mailings I threw away contained a reservation form for parking right behind my dorm the next semester. When I finally inquired about reserving a space a few months later, they informed me the lot was already filled. The closest lot I could get that semester was by the vet school about a half-mile away. It sucked! Read your mail."

—Adam, Journalism
University of Missouri,
Columbia

77 Get Involved

My first year at Harvard, I locked myself in my dorm room and did nothing but study. I was a total hermit! And while my grades were good, I didn't begin excelling academically until my sophomore year, when I came out of my shell and got more involved—involved in group studies, intramural soccer, aerobics classes, different social gatherings. I really believe getting involved helped me become a better, more well-rounded student."

—Laura, History
Harvard University

78 Find a New Roommate (if Necessary)

"Having a roommate is supposed to be part of the college learning experience, but sometimes it can make the learning experience difficult and miserable. My first year at UT, my roommate and I got along reasonably well. We weren't 'best friends' but we respected each other and did our best to stay out of the other's way. The roommate I was stuck with my sophomore year, however, was like someone straight out of the movie 'Animal House'—a complete slob who listened to loud acid rock and couldn't care less about his studies. After a couple weeks, I'd had it—I told my R.A. (resident adviser) that I needed to get out before I went postal. She set me up in a single room for the remainder of the semester. I don't know if it 'hurt my roommate's feelings' that I moved out, but I didn't care—I got a 3.9 that semester."

—Sri, Advertising
Ohio State University

79 Do Your Own Work

"Don't depend on anyone to bail you out, such as lending you class notes or typing your papers for you. I remember this one guy, Jason, who lived down the hall from me a few years ago. He knocked on my door one evening a few days before the final—he wanted to borrow my notes. He hardly went to class and was desperate. I told him to forget it, and I know another guy in our dorm told him the same thing. Most students have enough of their own work to do and problems to worry about. Things will go a lot smoother if you take responsibility for yourself and not rely on anyone else to bail you out."

—Shane, Psychology
University of Southern California

REALITY TELEVISION COMES FULL CIRCLE...

80 Limit TV Time

"One of the things that has helped me most is limiting my TV time. Television is such a waste—it mesmerizes you. It's so easy to lose track of time watching TV. Three hours in front of the tube can pass like 30 minutes. What I do is limit my TV watching when school's in session to just two of my favorite shows each week (*Extreme Makeover Home Edition* and *CSI: Miami*). When I started doing this, I was amazed at how much time this freed up for my studies."

—Sarah, Education
University of Northern Colorado

81 Rise and Shine

"What I do is schedule my classes early in the day, starting at around 8 a.m. I also make sure the hour after each class is free—I use this time study and review what was covered in the class before. This also ensures I'm not rushing from class to class. Since I'm not an 'early bird,' getting up at the crack of dawn is especially tough the first few weeks, but it gets easier once you get into the routine.

"I think there's also something to be said about the mere exercise of getting up early. When I get up and go for a run in the early morning, then eat a nutritious breakfast, I feel good; I feel energized! (On the contrary, I feel irritable and cranky when I sleep in.) Developing a healthy morning routine has definitely helped contribute to my success."

—Jennifer, Political Science
University of North Carolina,
Chapel Hill

82 Focus on Performing Well on Tests

"When you get down to it, your GPA is largely a result of how well you perform on tests. And I think being a good 'test taker' is as simple as knowing the material. Period. If you know the material, you'll do well on the test; if you don't, you won't.

"If you're having trouble understanding something, make sure to go see your professor or T.A. as many times as needed, for extra help, before the test. I never go into a test feeling even a little unsure of the material. Not to sound cocky, but by test time, I feel like a champion prizefighter—I know for a fact that I'm going to go in there and kick that test's ass! I even prepare myself like it's a prizefight—me against the test. I'll 'train' for weeks, studying, drilling, making sure I know the material upside-down and inside-out. Then, the night before, I'll get a good night's sleep; I'll then exercise early the next morning; eat a few good, healthy meals; review a little bit; listen to inspiring music the hour before the test... then it's on!"

—Brad, Premed
University of Florida,
Gainesville

83 Learn from Your Slip-ups

"If you 'bomb' a test or turn in a lousy paper, try to learn something positive from it. A few semesters ago, I enrolled in a lower-level biology class, thinking it was going to be an easy 'A.' I totally bombed the first test. The professor asked the stupidest, most insanely detailed questions. It was a good learning experience, though. I studied that test and got a good sense of the kind of crazy questions the professor liked to ask and how I needed to study in order to better prepare for future tests. I rebounded to earn an 'A' in the class."

—Kirsten, Biology
Arizona State University

84 Keep a Positive Attitude

"The best advice I can give is to maintain a positive attitude. I've noticed that so many students live in the 'negative zone'—they bemoan everything from university bureaucracy to their classes to their professors to their roommates to the weather. It's hard to be successful at anything with that kind of mindset. I don't know of any studies to support this, but I think there's a direct, positive correlation between attitude and GPA."

—Curtis, Advertising
University of Illinois

85 Get to Know Your Professors

"My number one key to college success? Get to know your professors. Go to office hours. Make sure they know your name and that getting an 'A' is a high priority for you. In fact, I know of a study carried out a few years ago by a researcher from Syracuse who found that the amount of interaction a student had with his or her professors was a significant predictor of academic success."

—Megan, Secondary Education
University of West Virginia

86 Develop a Routine

"For me, developing a daily routine that supports my goals is essential. I try to get into this routine as soon as school starts and then stick with it—for example, I try to study at the same time and place each weekday night. I like to go where other students are studying—it reminds me that I'm not the only one going through this. In a way, that's comforting."

—Shannon, Food Science
University of Oklahoma

CHAPTER 11

College Essentials: What You Need to Succeed

There are certain "essentials" every college student needs to succeed. While this list isn't all-encompassing, it's certainly a good start. Here's what I suggest you get...

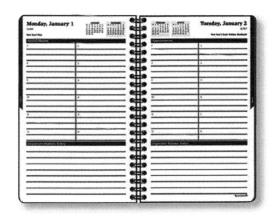

87 Daily Planner

Any college student who aspires to make the grade needs a daily planner to help keep track of tests, homework assignments, term-paper due dates, appointments and other important happenings. You don't need anything fancy or expensive. I like the At-A-Glance® Collegiate Daily Appointment Book, available at Staples (Staples.com) and other office supply stores for about $15. You can also find it, or something similar, at your university bookstore.

88 Alarm Clock

The fastest way into your professor's "dog house" is to show up late for class. I had a philosophy professor who literally ran a student out of the classroom for showing up late. When the poor sap walked through the door, the professor rushed up the steps, screaming at the student to get out. While most professors won't go to this extreme, many will stop class long enough to give you a good "stare down." Don't let this happen to you. Get yourself a reliable alarm clock. I like the Sony ICF-C212 FM/AM clock radio. This model, available for around $13 on Amazon.com, features inch-high green LED numerals for those who, like me, are useless without their contacts in, and the blaring alarm is sure to wake even the soundest of sleepers. What's more, this clock has a full-power back-up feature (9V battery required), which will keep your clock and alarm functions operational should a power outage occur.

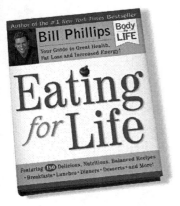

89 Eating *for* Life

Develop a spring-break body while nourishing optimal physical and cognitive health by embracing Bill Phillips' *New York Times* bestselling Eating *for* Life Program, available at Amazon.com for just over $20. This book, which I helped write (see page 350), features 150 nutritious, delicious, easy-to-follow recipes perfect for college students who don't have a lot of time to spend in the kitchen (or who don't even have a kitchen).

90 Nutrition Shakes & Blender

Nutrition shakes are the ideal food for busy college students. The better of these powdered nutritional formulas provide healthy amounts of the essential nutrients our bodies need to work right, including lean proteins, quality carbohydrates, essential fats, vitamins, minerals and water. They can be prepared in less than a minute in the comfort of your dorm room or bedroom, and at just a few bucks per serving, cost less than what you'd pay for a crummy fast-food burger and fries. I like Bill Phillips' Eating *for* Life Right brand of nutrition shakes (EatingRight.com), available at health-food stores like GNC and The Vitamin Shoppe. These shakes are a perfect complement to the Eating *for* Life program and taste just like delicious milkshakes. A shaker bottle can be used to mix up these shakes, but for best results, I recommend using a blender. Any ol' blender available at Target or Wal-Mart will do. They start at around $15.

91 iPod Mini

Research shows listening to uplifting music boosts both exercise and cognitive performance. What student wouldn't want to experience these effects? At under $200 at Amazon.com, Apple's new iPod Mini, which tips the scales at a featherweight 3.6 ounces and features 18 hours of battery life while holding upwards of 1,000 songs, is a sound investment or birthday "wish-list" item.

92 Filing System

From class schedules to grade tran-
scripts to bank statements to various documents and university mailings, college
students have piles of important papers
they need to keep track of. As soon as
you receive any paper or document you'd
rather not misplace or accidentally throw
away, you should file it away in a safe and
secure, easily accessible place. I like the
Black File Security Box, available at Target
for about $28. This transportable filing system
features inside metal rails to accommodate letter-size hanging file
folders, and the double key locks will keep nosey roommates from
digging through your stuff.

93 Mountain Bike

Trying to get around campus in your car is such a hassle—you're
constantly having to stop and wait for students to cross the street, and
there's hardly ever an available parking space close to your class.
Plus, the university parking patrol is always on the prowl, just itching to pass out tickets to vehicles improperly parked. If you live any-
where near campus, you're better off riding a bicycle. In fact, you'll
often get to class faster riding a bike than driving your car. Because
I always took off-road shortcuts through campus, my ride of choice
was a durable mountain bike. Any of the rugged but affordable "Jeep"
brand of mountain bikes available at Target is a solid choice.

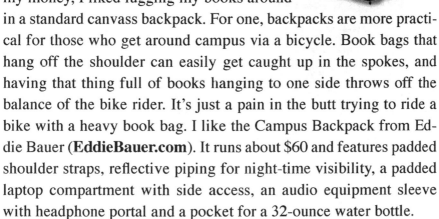

94 Campus Backpack

Stylish leather book bags like the law students have may look "cool," but for my money, I liked lugging my books around in a standard canvas backpack. For one, backpacks are more practical for those who get around campus via a bicycle. Book bags that hang off the shoulder can easily get caught up in the spokes, and having that thing full of books hanging to one side throws off the balance of the bike rider. It's just a pain in the butt trying to ride a bike with a heavy book bag. I like the Campus Backpack from Eddie Bauer (**EddieBauer.com**). It runs about $60 and features padded shoulder straps, reflective piping for night-time visibility, a padded laptop compartment with side access, an audio equipment sleeve with headphone portal and a pocket for a 32-ounce water bottle.

95 Dress-Casual Clothes

Looking like a "scrub" can not only negatively impact your grades (see Chapter 3), but it can wreck your social life, as well. Unless you either look like Brad Pitt or have a lot of money, most good-looking gals won't want to be seen with a guy who dresses like he's still in high school. And most guys who have it together, if given their druthers, would rather be seen with a fashionable gal. Next time you're at the mall and you see your favorite "T-shirt hut," keep walking—stores like the Gap have more of what you should be looking for.

96 Workout Gear

Take advantage of your student recreational facility. Hit the weights, take some aerobics classes, shoot hoops—get your butt in shape. Fit students not only have more active social lives, but it's a proven fact that they achieve better grades, as well. In a recent study of 954,000 California students, higher academic achievement was directly associated with higher levels of physical fitness.

"This statewide study provides compelling evidence that the physical well-being of students has a direct impact on their ability to achieve academically," said Delaine Eastin, California State Superintendent of Public Instruction. "We now have the proof we've been looking for: Students achieve best when they are physically fit. Thousands of years ago, the Greeks understood the importance of improving spirit, mind and body. The research presented here validates their philosophic approach with scientific validation."

From brand-name running shoes to microfiber activewear, stores like Kohl's and Target have an affordable selection of quality workout gear to choose from.

97 The World Almanac

No student should go without a good almanac filled with all kinds of facts, statistics, lists, charts, graphs, maps and other nuggets of information. Go with *The World Almanac and Book of Facts*, which is updated annually and available on Amazon.com for about $10. *The Los Angeles Times* calls *The World Almanac* "the most useful reference book known to modern man."

98 As a Man Thinketh

Check out the "recommended reading list" of just about any successful person, and you'll probably find this little book written over a hundred years ago by philosopher James Allen. It will open your eyes to the undisputable truth that we are the makers of ourselves and our destiny by virtue of the thoughts we harbor. Order it new on Amazon.com for about $8—it'll be the best 8 bucks you'll ever spend.

99 Savings Account

Under the mattress of your bed isn't exactly the best place for your spending money, let alone your tuition funds. As soon as you arrive on campus, head for your nearest bank and open a savings and checking account. Talk with one of the bankers to see which kind of account will work best for you. Becoming financially educated and responsible is an essential skill set for any student.

> **TIP:** Use cash, not your credit card, for personal spending. There's no surer way to future financial ruin than racking up massive credit card debt, especially as a student. Research shows people don't spend nearly as much when they use cash as opposed to a credit card.

100 A Good Watch

The odds of you showing up to class on time, or at all, aren't very good if you don't even know what time it is. Instead of guesstimating or constantly bugging others for the time, take some responsibility and invest in a good watch. Eddie Bauer (**EddieBauer.com**) has a good selection of fashionable watches for both guys and gals.

CHAPTER 12

The BIG Secret to College Success

101 Want It

The *Rocky* films... you've seen those, right? Probably not all 15 of them but at least enough to get an idea about what the "Italian Stallion" was all about. So what was it about this guy that made him special? What was it that endeared him so to moviegoers? That had us pulling and cheering for him as if he were true to life? Was it his Muhammad Ali moves? His Sugar Ray Leonard speed? His Rocky Marciano right cross?

No, No and No (in that order).

For the most part, the guy was a human punching bag, right? A palooka who got his brains beat in from the opening bell. But he had an iron chin and the iron will to go with it. He was the quintessential underdog who scratched and clawed his way to the top on pure grit and guts. In the films, Mickey, Rock's crusty old trainer, called this hunger, this insatiable fighting spirit, "The eye of the tiger." It was *this* quality, not speed, punching power or pizzazz, that tugged at our heartstrings and made Rocky a film hero for the ages.

In writing the original Rocky script, Sylvester Stallone is said to have based the character on a real-life, never-give-up, two-bit boxer/ bleeder by the name of Chuck Wepner, but it just as well could have been based on Sly himself.

In 1975, Stallone, a frustrated, unemployed, unknown actor, watched Wepner fight for Muhammad Ali's heavyweight crown on closed-circuit television. Wepner almost went the distance. He even knocked Ali down. The fight was stopped with 19 seconds left in the 15th round. Wepner was beaten and bloodied, but the heart he showed won over the crowd. They went crazy. So did Stallone. He rushed home and scribbled out the screenplay that became Rocky in 86 hours.

A studio wanted to buy the script but was not about to cast a small-time actor like Stallone in the starring role. Burt Reynolds and Robert Redford were two names the studio expressed interest in. But Stallone would have nothing of it. "There comes a crossroad in your life," he wrote in a 1999 *Newsweek* column. "I said, 'This is my story, and I'm so used to being broke that I am willing to go down with the ship, and insist on starring in it.'"

The numbers offered for the script rose steadily, going from $20,000 to $100,000 to $360,000 (the equivalent of a $2 million script today)—all contingent on an A-list actor starring as Rocky. "So I did a lot more soul-searching," says Stallone. "Intellectually, you're a fool if you don't take the money. But emotionally, I said, 'Could I live with myself for the rest of my life knowing I sold off the script and didn't stay with the project?'"

The answer he finally came to was no. He stuck to his guns.

The studio finally agreed to cast Stallone, but with a flood of contingencies. They paid pennies on the dollar for the screenplay, and the movie had to be made in only 28 days and for under $1 million. "It was down to the bare bones," says Stallone. "Everyone worked for, like, $360 a week. I put everyone in it. I put my dog, my brother, my father—anyone who would work for free was in that movie. I wore my own wardrobe and changed in the back of a station wagon. Just a few months before, I had had to sell my dog because I couldn't afford to keep him. And then when the movie finally came along, I had to try to buy my dog back. The other family had owned it for six months; they weren't exactly thrilled, but I said, 'Please... this dog belongs in the movie. He had suffered along with me for two years.' I said, '*Please* let him have a shot in the movie.'"

In 1976, the film, with Stallone's dog, Bupkes, playing a starring role, took the Academy Awards by storm, winning Oscars for Best Picture, Director and Editing. Stallone even garnered a nomination for Best Actor. Like the character he created, Sly, a product himself of the Philadelphia slums, had a dream and fought for it with all his heart and soul.

"Yeah, that's great," you might be thinking. "Good for Sly. But what does this have to do with getting good grades in college?"

Well, in a word... *everything.*

You see, all the tips and techniques, secrets and strategies in the world ain't worth a damn if you don't really want it. You've gotta want to succeed. Governor Arnold Schwarzenegger has called this special quality *want power.* It's this attribute, more than anything else, that is the foundation for achievement in school, business, just about any endeavor you can think of.

The governor's life could be a case study of what can happen when a clear vision for the future is infused with an intense desire to achieve it. As a boy growing up in Austria, Arnold dreamed of coming to America and doing great things. "I had a vision when I was a kid, and I went after that vision, after that goal, after that dream, and I would not let go until it was accomplished," he says. First he dreamed of becoming the best bodybuilder in the world. After he realized it, he dreamed of becoming an "A-list" Hollywood actor. After he realized that, this ambitious immigrant who could barely speak English when he came to America at age 21 dreamed of becoming governor of the Golden State. Now speculation is Gov. Schwarzenegger has his sights set on the White House. Some say that's impossible. Knowing this man's superhuman want power, I certainly wouldn't put it past him.

Speaking of impossible, that's what people told Mina Hobbi five years ago when she said she'd one day have a lean, toned body. At the time, the 44-year-old was morbidly obese, carrying some 200-plus pounds on her 5-foot-1-inch frame. She says the extra weight made her life a living hell—in addition to migraines and ulcers, she fell into a deep depression and even contemplated suicide.

She had tried again and again to lose the weight. Each failed attempt only fed her frustration. Then one day Mina found inspiration in the success stories shared in a magazine for which I served as editor-in-chief called *Muscle Media*. Mina says reading these uplifting, true stories of transformation caused a tectonic shift in her thinking. Instead of dwelling on how bad things were, she started dreaming about how *great things could be.* That sparked desire. The more she visualized, the more she wanted it. She made the decision to succeed at rebuilding her body.

"I wrote a contract with myself to lose the weight in 366 days because it was a leap year," says Mina. "I knew that I was going to fall down along the way, but this time I decided that when I fall down, I'm going to get up and dust myself off and keep on going."

She explains that the first time she went to the gym, she literally became lodged in one of the exercise machines. The humiliation she felt would've been enough to knock most people down for the count, but Mina's desire to change was so intense that nothing was going to stop her. True to her contract, she got up, dusted herself off and began exercising on the beach near her home in Hawaii.

"I had a long way to go, but I stuck with it one day at a time," she says. "Walking and running along the beach; nutrition shakes and healthy foods and water; setting goals, planning, keeping a journal… I worked hard to do all these new things. And then the desire paid off: People started encouraging and complimenting me! That inspired me to keep going!"

After 366 days, Mina had lost 85 pounds of unhealthy bodyweight. She not only achieved the "impossible"—having the lean, toned body she dreamed of—but now she's a certified fitness coach, helping others achieve their own transformations.

"I have a level of energy, self-confidence and personal strength now that I never knew existed in me," says Mina. "And I'm now sharing that with others who, like me, have struggled with obesity."

Rest assured, the techniques you've learned in this book are breakthrough and will help you get good grades in college. But before you begin applying them, ask yourself how badly you want it. When times get tough and temptation knocks you to the canvass, do you have the want power to pull yourself up and keep going? Or, is doing well in college something that's just not worth fighting for? Maybe being "average" is good enough. The mere fact that you're reading this book, however, tells me that you're dedicated to being better than the "average Joe" or "Jane."

Think about how badly you *really* want it. While I cannot automatically grant you "want power," I can share that doing well in college is one of the best things you could ever do to set yourself up for future success. Plus, there's just something to be said for seeing "A's" on your transcript. It's black-and-white validation that you are, indeed, better than average.

In this book, I've shown you the way. Now it's your turn to bring it to life by infusing it with the *want*. I wish you the very best of success in college and beyond, and please, if you have any questions, comments or if you'd simply like to share your successes, as well as setbacks, with others who've made the same decision you have, please visit our online community at **www.HowToAceCollege.com**. I look forward to hearing from you!

APPENDIX A

Do You Make These Common Errors in English?

If you think running a simple "spell check" on your paper is sufficient for catching most booboos and blunders, you've got another thing coming. Fact is, misspellings make up just a small portion of the mountain of grammatical mistakes college students make. Following is some of the more common foul-ups...

Using the Wrong Preposition

as to: *not* as for
comply with: *not* comply to
contrast to: *not* contrast with
as to: *not* as for
convince of or that: *not* convince to
die of: *not* die with or die from
different from: *not* different than
identical with: *not* identical to
independent of: *not* independent from
investigation of: *not* investigation into
persuade to: *not* persuade of or persuade that
plead guilty of (a crime): *not* plead guilty to
pleased (at, by) a gift: *not* pleased with a gift
put into words: *not* put in words
speak with: *not* speak to
talk with: *not* talk to

Other Wrong Words in a Phrase

adopt a resolution: *not* pass
again and again: *not* over and over
as good as: *not* equally good as
be sure to: *not* be sure and
compared with: *not* as compared with
decide whether: *not* decide if
doubt that: *not* doubt if
on each side: *not* on either side
red-haired person: *not* red-headed person
    (a person is red-haired; a bird may be red-headed)
safe-deposit box: *not* safety-deposit box

Errors with Similar-Sounding Words

anchors aweigh: *not* anchors away
champing at the bit: *not* chomping
heartrending: *not* heart-rendering
run a gantlet: *not* gauntlet
stamping grounds: *not* stomping
tinker's dam: *not* damn
toe the line: *not* tow
well-heeled: *not* healed
wet your whistle: *not* whet
whet your appetite: *not* wet
wet your pants: *not* whet
    (just making sure you're still with me here ☺)
wreak havoc: *not* wreck

Errors in Grammar

can only: *not* cannot help but
cannot help: *not* cannot help but
couldn't care less: *not* could care less
couldn't help: *not* couldn't help but
either... or: *not* either... nor
I hope: *not* I would hope
more important: *not* more importantly
neither is: *not* neither are

Other Common Blunders

a lot: *not* alot
affect/effect: *Affect* is a verb meaning "to influence"; *effect* is a noun meaning "result" and a verb meaning "to cause."
blond/blonde, brunet/brunette: The forms *without* the final "e" are used as the adjective applying to either a man or a woman or as a noun applying to men only. The forms *with* the "e" on the end are used only as nouns applying to women, although many women find these terms offensive and blatantly sexist.
centers on: *not* centers around
compare to/compare with: Use *compare to* when similarities are emphasized; use *compare with* when differences are emphasized.
convince/persuade: You're *convinced that* or *convinced of* something, but you're *persuaded to* do something.
farther/further: *Farther* is used for literal distance, such as farther down the road; *further* is used for figurative distance, such as further into a subject.

fewer/less: Use *less* to modify singular words, *fewer* to modify plural words. Keep in mind that a word plural in form is sometimes singular in concept, as when dollars or pounds refer to a set amount as opposed to individual units. Use *fewer* with items that would take many, *less* with items that would take much: He weighs less than 200 pounds because 200 pounds is how *much* he weighs, not how many.

half-mast/half-staff: Flags are lowered, not raised, to *half-staff* on land, *half-mast* only on a ship or naval base.

its/it's: *Its* is the possessive pronoun; *it's* is the contraction for *it is*.

lay/lie: *Lay* is a transitive verb meaning "to set something down"; its principal parts are lay, laid, have laid, laying. *Lie* is an intransitive verb meaning "to rest"; its principal parts are lie, lay, have lain, lying.

lead/led: *Lead* is the main present-tense form of the verb to lead and also the name of an element that used to be put in gasoline; the past tense of the verb *lead* is *led*, not lead.

premiere: Use only as a noun, not as a verb. Don't write that a play will premiere but that it will have its premiere.

raise/rise: *Raise* is a transitive verb meaning "to lift" something; its principal parts are raise, raised, have raised, raising. Rise is an intransitive verb meaning "get up"; its principal parts are rise, rose, have risen and rising.

that/which: Use *that* to introduce restrictive (essential) clauses that do not require commas, *which* to introduce nonrestrictive (nonessential) clauses that do require commas.

who/whom, whoever/whomever: *Who* and *whoever* are nominative-case pronouns; *whom* and *whomever* are objective-case pronouns. An easy way to make sure you use each pair properly is to begin reading a sentence after the choice between *who/whom* or *who-ever/whomever*, adding either *he* or *him* to complete the thought; if *he* works better, use *who* or *whoever*; if him works better, use *whom* or *whomever.* For example: *Who* did you say aced the test? (Did you say *he* aced the test?)

who's/whose: *Who's* is the contraction for *who is*; *whose* is the possessive form of the pronoun *who.*

SOURCE: *Working with Words: A Concise Handbook for Media Writers and Editors,* Second Edition. New York: St. Martin's Press, Inc., 1993. Brian S. Brooks & James L. Pinson.

APPENDIX B

Do You Lack "Style" in Your Writing?

One of the most widespread mistakes made by college students is writing without any sort of style. When I say most students lack style, I don't mean their writing isn't "chic" or fashionable — I mean it's *inconsistent*. They'll use the numeral 9 in some instances and spell it out (nine) in others; they'll spell out some state names (California) while abbreviating others (Fla.); they'll capitalize formal titles in front of some names (President Bush) and fail to do so in front of others (coach Roy Williams). Professors are sticklers for this and take great delight in marking off points for any inconsistencies they might find.

As a journalist, I follow the style set forth in the *Associated Press Stylebook*. It's the style used by most newspapers and magazines. It's also an appropriate style to follow when writing papers for most classes. If your professor prefers you follow another style (APA style, for example), make sure you follow that instead. *Always* ask your professor which style he or she prefers you use.

Following is a summary of the style rules set forth by the AP.

Abbreviations and Acronyms

1. Punctuations and abbreviations
- Generally speaking, abbreviations of two letters or fewer use periods: 700 B.C., 8 a.m., U.N., U.S., R.I., N.Y. Exceptions: AM radio, FM radio, 35 mm camera, IQ, TV.
- Generally speaking, abbreviations of three letters or more do not use periods: CIA, FBI, NATO, mpg, mph. Exception: c.o.d.

2. Symbols
- Always write out *%* as *percent* in a paper.
- Always write out *&* as *and* unless it is an actual part of a company's formal name.
- Always use the symbol *$* rather than the word *dollar* with any actual figure, and put the symbol before the figure. Write out *dollar* only if you are speaking of, say, the value of the dollar on the world market.

3. Dates
- Never abbreviate days of the week.
- Don't abbreviate a month unless it has a date of the month with it: August; August 2005; Aug. 7; Aug. 7, 2005.
- The five months spelled with five letters or fewer are never abbreviated: March; April 20; May 25, 2005; June 2005; July of that year.
- Never abbreviate *Christmas* as *Xmas*.
- Fourth of July is written out.

4. People and titles
- The abbreviations Gov., Lt. Gov., Rep., Sen., the Rev. and military titles are used on first reference, then the title is dropped on subsequent references. Some titles not abbreviated before a name: Attorney General, District Attorney, President, Professor and Superintendent.
- The abbreviations Jr. and Sr. are used behind a name on first reference if appropriate, but they are not set off by commas.

5. Organizations
- The first reference for most organizations is written out in full rather than using an acronym: National Organization for Women.

For CIA, FBI and GOP, however, the acronym may be used on first reference.

- Do not put the abbreviation of an organization in parentheses behind the full name on first reference.
- The abbreviations Co., Cos., Corp., Inc. and Ltd. Are used at the end of a company's name even if the company spells the word out; they are not abbreviated if followed by other words such as "of America."
- Political affiliations are abbreviated after a name in the following way: *Sen. John McCain, R-Ariz., said...* Note the use of a single letter without a period for the party and the use of commas around the party and state.
- The word *association* is never abbreviated, even as part of a name.

6. Places

- Don't abbreviate a state name unless it follows the name of a city in that state: Colorado; Boulder, Colo.
- The six states spelled with five letters or fewer are never abbreviated, nor are the two noncontiguous states: Alaska, Hawaii, Idaho, Iowa, Maine, Ohio, Texas, Utah.
- State abbreviations used are the old-fashioned ones, not the post office's two-letter ones: Colo., *not* CO. Below are the abbreviations to use:

Ala.	Kan.	Neb.	R.I.
Ariz.	Ky.	Nev.	S.C.
Ark.	La.	N.H.	S.D.
Calif.	Md.	N.J.	Tenn.
Colo.	Mass.	N.M.	Vt.
Conn.	Mich.	N.Y.	Wash.

(continued on next page)

Del.	Minn.	N.C.	W.Va.
Fla.	Miss.	N.D.	Wis.
Ga.	Mo.	Okla.	Wyo.
Ill.	Mont.	Ore.	
Ind.	Neb.	Pa.	

- The names of thoroughfares are not abbreviated if there is no street address with them: Main Street; Century Boulevard West.
- If the thoroughfare's name has the words *avenue, boulevard, street* or any of the directions on a map, such as north or southeast, those words are abbreviated with a street address: 711 W. Golden St., 1822 Jackson Blvd., 140 Durham Ave.
- In a highway's name, U.S. is always abbreviated, but a state's name never is. In the case of an interstate highway, the name is written in full on first reference, abbreviated on subsequent ones: Interstate 70 (first reference), I-70 (second reference).
- *Fort* and *Mount* are never abbreviated. The abbreviation *St.* for *Saint* is always used in place of names, however, with the exception of Saint John in New Brunswick, Ste. Genevieve in Missouri and Sault Ste. Marie in Michigan and Ontario.
- Abbreviate United States and United Nations as U.S. and U.N. when used as adjectives, but spell them out as nouns.

7. Miscellaneous

- IQ: No periods.
- No. 1, No.2, etc. Abbreviate and capitalize the word *number* when followed by a numeral.
- TV: No periods.
- vs.: Don't abbreviate versus as v.

Capitalization

1. General rule: Proper nouns are capitalized; common nouns are not.

- With animals, food and plants, capitalize only the parts of a compound name that would be capitalized by themselves: German shepherd, basset hound; Boston cream pie, Dutch elm. Exceptions: brussels sprouts, french fries, graham crackers, manhattan cocktail.
- Beware of trade names that are often mistakenly used generically: Band-Aid, Coke, Crock-Pot, Fiberglas, Frisbee, Jeep, Jell-O, Kleenex, Q-Tip, Realtor, Scotch tape, Seeing Eye dog, Styrofoam, Vaseline, Velcro, Xerox.

2. Regions are capitalized, but directions are not:

- We drove east two miles to catch the interstate out West.
- Adjectives and nouns pertaining to a region are capitalized: Southern accent, Western movie, a Southerner, a Western.
- A region combined with a country's name is not capitalized unless that is the name of a divided country: eastern United States, North Korea.
- A region combined with a state name is capitalized only if it is famous: Southern California, southern Colorado.

3. When two or more compound proper nouns are combined to share a word in common made plural, the shared plural is lowercase:

- Missouri and Mississippi rivers; Broomfield and Legacy high schools.

4. Government and college terms are not always consistent:

- Departments. College departments follow the animal, food and plant rule, capitalizing only words already proper nouns in themselves: Spanish department, sociology department. But a specific government department is always capitalized, even without the city, state or federal designator, and even if turned around with *of* deleted: Police Department, Fire Department, State Department.
- Committees. College and government committees are capitalized if the formal name is given rather than a shorter, descriptive designation: Special Senate Select Committee to Investigate Improper Labor-Management Practices; rackets committee.
- Degrees. Academic degrees are spelled out and lowercase: bachelor of arts degree, master's degree. Avoid the abbreviations Ph.D., M.A., B.A., etc., except in lists.
- Always capitalized (unless plural or generic): City Council, County Commission (but alone, council and commission are lowercase). Cabinet is always capitalized when referring to advisers. Legislature is capitalized if the state's body is formally named that. Capitol, the building, is always capitalized, but capital, the city, is not.
- Never capitalized: board of directors, board of trustees (but Board of Curators and Board of Education are capitalized). Federal, government and administration are not capitalized. President and vice president are capitalized only before a name.
- Military titles (Sgt. Maj., Gen.) before a name are capitalized, as are Air Force, Army, Marines and Navy if referring to U.S. forces.
- Political parties are capitalized, including the word party: Democratic Party, Socialist Party. Be sure, however, to capitalize words like communist, democratic, fascist and socialist only if they refer to a formal party rather than a philosophy.

5. Religion:

- Lowercase *pope* unless before a name, but *Mass* is always uppercase. Pronouns for God or Jesus are lowercase.
- Bible is capitalized if meaning the Holy Scriptures and lowercased when referring to another book: a hunter's bible.
- Sacraments are capitalized if they commemorate events in the life of Jesus or signify his presence: baptism, Communion.

6. Formal titles of people are capitalized before a name, but occupational titles are not:

- President Bush, Mayor John Smith, Coach Larry Brown, astronaut Joe Rogan.

Numerals

1. Cardinal numbers (numerals) are used in:

- Addresses. Always use numerals for street addresses: 1711 N. 10th St.
- Ages. Always use numerals, even for days or months: 3 days old; John Smith, 55.
- Aircraft and spacecraft: F-4, DC-10, Apollo 11; exception: Air Force One.
- Clothes size: size 6
- Dates. Always use the numeral alone—no -rd, -st or -th behind it.
- Dimensions: 5-foot-6-inch guard (but no hyphen when the word modified is one associated with size, such as 3 feet tall, 10 feet long).
- Highways: U.S. 63

- Millions, billions and trillions use a numeral before the word: 1.2 billion.
- Money. Always use numerals, but starting with a million, write like this: $1.4 million.
- Percentages. Always use numerals except at the beginning of a sentence.
- Recipes. Even amounts of less than 10 take numerals.
- Speeds: 55 mph, 4 knots
- Sports. Use numerals for just about everything: score 8-6, 2 yards, 3-under-par, 2 strokes.
- Temperatures. All are numerals but zero; below zero, spell out minus: minus 7.
- Time: 4 a.m., 7:11 p.m.; but noon, midnight, five minutes, three hours.
- Weights: 7 pounds, 11 ounces
- Years. Use numerals without commas: A date is the only numeral that can start a sentence: 1988 was a good year; decade of the '80s

2. Numerals with the suffixes -nd, -rd and -th are used for:
- Political divisions (precincts, wards, districts): 3rd Congressional District
- Military sequences: 1st Lt., 2nd Division, 7th Fleet
- Courts: 2nd District Court; 10th Circuit Court of Appeals
- Streets after Ninth: For First through Ninth, use words: Fifth Avenue, 11th Street.
- Amendments to the Constitution after Ninth: For First through Ninth, use words.

3. Words are used instead of numerals for:
- Numbers of less than 10, not excepted above.

- Any number at the start of a sentence except for a year.
- Casual numbers: about a hundred or so.
- Fractions less than one: one-half.

4. Mixed numerals are used for fractions greater than one:
- 1½

5. Roman numerals are used for a man who is the third or later in his family to bear a name, and for a king, queen, pope or world war:
- John D. Rockefeller III, Pope John Paul II, Queen Elizabeth II, World War I.

SOURCE: *Working with Words: A Concise Handbook for Media Writers and Editors, Second Edition.* New York: St. Martin's Press, Inc., 1993. Brian S. Brooks & James L. Pinson.